Prophet Muhammad's Hadith Stories for Kids

Understanding Islam Through The Prophet's Teachings

Aasma S.

My First Picture Book Inc.

Copyright © 2024 by My First Picture Book Inc.

All rights reserved.

No portion of this book may be reproduced in any form without written permission from the publisher or author, except as permitted by U.S. copyright law.

Contents

Introduction	1
1. The Honest Merchant	4
2. The Kind Neighbor	8
3. The Trustworthy Friend	12
4. The Generous Heart	16
5. The Patient Farmer	20
6. The Compassionate Brother	24
7. The Brave Boy	28
8. The Thankful Child	32
9. The Respectful Student	36
10. The Polite Visitor	40
11. The Truthful Girl	44

12.	The Forgiving Friend	48
13.	The Fair Judge	52
14.	The Loving Parent	56
15.	The Curious Learner	60
16.	The Humble Leader	64
17.	The Gentle Shepherd	68
18.	The Responsible Child	72
19.	The Faithful Believer	76
20.	The Cheerful Helper	80
21.	The Sincere Worshipper	84
22.	The Generous Host	88
23.	The Patient Mother	92
24.	The Grateful Son	96
25.	The Honest Worker	100
26.	The Gentle Friend	104
27.	The Caring Nurse	108

28. The Respectful Neighbor	112
29. The Brave Protector	116
30. The Truthful Witness	120
31. The Kind Teacher	124
32. The Patient Fisherman	130
33. The Grateful Traveler	134
34. The Responsible Gardener	140
35. The Joyful Journey of Learning	144
36. The Humble Scholar	148
37. The Just King	152
38. The Generous Farmer	156
39. The Compassionate Nurse	160
40. The Brave Soldier	164
41. The Patient Tailor	168
42. The Grateful Farmer	172
43. The Responsible Student	176

44. The Cheerful Neighbor	180
45. The Humble Artisan	184
46. The Loving Friend	188
47. The Just Judge	192
48. The Kind Cook and the Hungry People	196
49. The Honest Farmer	202
50. The Brave Leader	208

Introduction

Dear Young Readers,

Welcome to "Prophet Muhammad's Hadith for Kids"! In this special book, you will discover beautiful teachings from our beloved Prophet Muhammad (Sallallahu Alayhi Wasallam). A Hadith is a saying or action of the Prophet that teaches us how to live a good and kind life. The Prophet Muhammad (Sallallahu Alayhi Wasallam) shared many wise words that help us understand how to be the best we can be — by being kind, honest, patient, and helpful to others.

This book is filled with stories that bring these Hadiths to life. Each story shows how these teachings can guide us in our everyday lives, just as they did for people long ago. Through these stories, you will learn how to make good choices, show love and respect to others, and find happiness in doing what is right.

As you read, remember that these teachings are like precious jewels that light up our hearts and make us better people. We hope this book inspires you to follow the beautiful example of the Prophet Muhammad (Sallallahu Alayhi Wasallam) and to always do good, be kind, and make the world a better place for everyone.

Happy reading and learning!

Chapter 1

The Honest Merchant

Once upon a time, in the village of Hadiya, lived a young boy named Ali. Ali was kind and loved by everyone. His father, Hassan, was a merchant who sold fruits and vegetables at the village market. Every day, Ali watched his father work hard and treat his customers with respect.

One morning, Hassan said, "Ali, you are old enough to help me at the market. You can learn to be a merchant too." Ali was excited to help his father and learn about selling fruits and vegetables.

At the market, Hassan showed Ali how to set up their stall. They placed the apples, oranges, and bananas neatly and arranged the vegetables in colorful rows. "Ali, always be honest with the customers," Hassan said. "If you are honest, people will trust you." Ali nodded and promised to be honest.

Ali watched his father carefully. Whenever a customer came, Hassan greeted them with a smile. He weighed the fruits and vegetables carefully and told them the correct price. If a fruit wasn't fresh, Hassan would let the customer know and offer a better one.

One day, Hassan had to leave the market early for a meeting in another village. "Ali, take care of the stall today," he said. "Remember to be honest and treat everyone well." Ali felt nervous but proud. He promised to do his best.

The first customer was an old lady who wanted some apples. Ali picked the best apples, weighed them, and told her the price. "Thank you, young man," she said. "These apples look delicious." Ali smiled, feeling more confident.

Next, a man came to buy potatoes. Ali weighed them and gave the correct price. The man smiled and said, "You are a good boy, Ali. Your father must be proud of you." Ali felt happy and continued to serve customers with honesty and kindness.

Later, a rich man came to the stall. He wanted to buy many oranges. Ali picked the best oranges and weighed them. The rich man frowned and said, "These oranges are not good. Give me better ones."

Ali replied, "Sir, these are very good, but if you don't like them, I can pick others." The rich man grew angry and said, "Do you think I am lying? These oranges are bad. Give me new ones, or I won't buy anything!"

Ali felt scared but remembered his father's words. He said, "Sir, I'm sorry, but these are the best oranges we have. I cannot lie to you."

The rich man stared at Ali, then smiled. "You are an honest boy," he said. "I like that. I will buy these oranges and come back again."

Ali felt relieved and happy. He thanked the rich man, knowing he had done the right thing. When Hassan returned, he saw the stall was nearly empty. "Ali, you did a great job today," he said. "I am proud of you."

Ali smiled and replied, "I remembered your words, Father. Honesty is the best policy." From that day on, Ali always helped his father and was honest with everyone.

Moral of the Story:

Always be honest. Honesty builds trust and respect, and it guides the path to righteousness and Paradise.

Hadith:

The Prophet Muhammad (Sallallahu Alayhi Wasallam) said: "Truthfulness leads to righteousness, and righteousness leads to Paradise. A man continues to tell the truth until he becomes a truthful person. Falsehood leads to wickedness and evil-doing, and wickedness leads to the Hellfire, and a man may continue to tell lies until he is written before Allah as a liar." (Sahih Muslim, Hadith 2607)

Chapter 2

The Kind Neighbor

Once upon a time, in a small village called Darakht, lived a young girl named Layla. Layla was happy and kind. She loved playing with her friends and helping her family. Layla had a special friend, Mrs. Zahra, an elderly woman who lived alone. Mrs. Zahra was always kind and had a warm smile.

One sunny morning, Layla's mother said, "Layla, I need you to go to Mrs. Zahra's house. She might need help with her chores." Layla loved visiting Mrs. Zahra and quickly got ready. When she arrived, Mrs. Zahra was sitting on her porch, knitting a scarf. She smiled when she saw Layla.

"Good morning, Mrs. Zahra!" Layla said. "Do you need any help today?"

Mrs. Zahra's eyes twinkled. "Oh, Layla, you are such a sweet girl. Yes, I could use some help. My garden needs watering, and I have some clothes that need washing."

Layla smiled, rolled up her sleeves, and got to work. First, she watered the garden, making sure every plant had enough water. The flowers seemed to smile as she cared for them. Then, she washed the clothes and hung them up to dry.

Mrs. Zahra watched her with a smile. "You are doing a wonderful job, Layla. I am so grateful."

Layla felt proud. "I like helping you, Mrs. Zahra. You are like a grandmother to me."

Mrs. Zahra's eyes filled with happy tears. "And you are like a granddaughter to me," she replied. "You have a very kind heart."

Layla continued helping Mrs. Zahra with other chores. She swept the floor, dusted the shelves, and even helped bake cookies. The house smelled wonderful. When it was time to go home, Mrs. Zahra gave Layla a big hug. "Thank you, Layla. You have made my day so much brighter."

Layla hugged her back. "I will come and help you again soon," she promised.

On her way home, Layla felt happy inside. She loved helping others. She told her mother about her day. "I helped Mrs. Zahra, and she was so happy," Layla said.

Her mother smiled. "I am proud of you, Layla. It is good to be kind and help others."

Layla nodded. She remembered the Prophet Muhammad's (peace be upon him) teaching: "He is not a believer who eats his fill while his neighbor is hungry." Layla understood the importance of being kind to neighbors.

From that day, Layla made sure to help Mrs. Zahra and other neighbors whenever they needed it. She helped carry groceries, swept porches, and read stories to younger children. Layla became known as the kindest girl in the village.

Moral of the Story:

Always be kind and helpful to your neighbors. Kindness makes the world a better place.

Hadith:

The Prophet Muhammad (Sallallahu Alayhi Wasallam) said: "Jibril kept recommending me to treat my neighbors kindly and politely so much so that I thought he would order me to make them my heirs." (Sahih Bukhari, Hadith 6014)

Chapter 3

The Trustworthy Friend

Once upon a time, in a small village called Amana, lived two best friends, Farid and Hamid. They were always together, playing, studying, and helping their families. Their bond was strong, and they often promised to support each other no matter what.

One sunny afternoon, while playing in the village square, they saw an old man struggling with a heavy sack of grains. Farid rushed to help him, and Hamid quickly followed. Together, they carried the sack to the old man's house.

"Thank you, boys," said the old man with a smile. "It's wonderful to see friends helping each other and others in need."

On their way back, Farid said, "Let's promise always to help each other and keep our word."

Hamid agreed, "I promise, Farid, to always help you and keep my word."

The next day at school, their teacher, Mr. Hakim, announced a competition. "Next week, each class will prepare a project. I need two volunteers to lead ours."

Farid and Hamid, excited about the opportunity, volunteered. "We'd like to lead the project!" Farid said eagerly.

Mr. Hakim smiled. "I trust you both to do a great job."

The two friends decided to build a model of their village and worked hard, gathering materials and drawing plans. But a few days later, Hamid fell ill and couldn't continue.

Farid went to visit Hamid, who was lying in bed. "I'm sorry, Farid," Hamid said, "I can't help with the project. I'm too sick."

Farid felt worried but remembered their promise. "Don't worry, Hamid. I'll finish the project for both of us. You just get better."

For the next few days, Farid worked tirelessly, staying up late to complete the project. Even without Hamid's help, he was determined to keep his promise.

Finally, the day of the competition arrived. Farid presented their completed model, a beautiful and detailed representation of their village. Everyone admired it, including Mr. Hakim.

"Excellent work, Farid!" said Mr. Hakim. "Where is Hamid?"

"He is still sick," Farid replied, "but we promised to help each other, so I finished it for both of us."

The results were announced, and their class won first place! Farid hurried to Hamid's house to share the news. "We won!" he exclaimed. "Our project was a success!"

Hamid's eyes lit up. "Thank you, Farid, for keeping your promise."

Farid smiled. "We are best friends, and we keep our promises."

From that day on, their friendship grew stronger, known as the most trustworthy in the village.

Moral of the Story:

Always keep your promises. Being trustworthy builds strong friendships and trust.

Hadith:

The Prophet Muhammad (Sallallahu Alayhi Wasallam) said: "The signs of a hypocrite are three: whenever he speaks, he tells a lie; whenever he promises, he breaks it; and whenever he is trusted, he betrays his trust." (Sahih Bukhari, Hadith 6094)

Chapter 4

The Generous Heart

Once upon a time, in a small village called Mehr, lived a young boy named Samir. He was a kind and cheerful boy who loved going to school and playing with his friends. Every day, Samir's mother packed him a delicious lunch, always ensuring he had enough food.

One sunny morning, Samir woke up excited for school. After getting ready, his mother handed him his lunchbox with a smile. "Enjoy your lunch, my dear," she said.

"Thank you, Mama!" Samir replied, hugging her before hurrying off to school.

At school, Samir's best friend was a boy named Amir. They sat together in class and played during recess. When lunchtime came, they sat under a big shady tree, and Samir eagerly opened his lunchbox, revealing his favorite foods: a sandwich, an apple, and cookies.

Just as Samir was about to take a bite, he noticed a boy sitting alone on a bench nearby. It was Karim, a new student in their class, who looked sad and hungry. Samir felt sympathy for Karim and remembered his mother's words about being kind and generous.

"Amir," Samir whispered, "Karim doesn't have any lunch. Let's help him."

Amir nodded. "You're right. Let's share our lunch."

Samir walked over to Karim and said with a smile, "Hi, Karim. Would you like to join us for lunch? We have plenty to share."

Karim looked surprised but grateful. "Really? Thank you. I didn't bring any lunch today."

Samir led Karim to their spot under the tree. He gave Karim half of his sandwich and a cookie, while Amir shared his apple. The three boys sat together, eating and chatting about their favorite games.

Karim's face brightened with happiness. "Thank you, Samir and Amir," he said. "You are very kind. I was so hungry."

Samir smiled warmly. "I'm glad we could help. It's nice to share with friends."

After lunch, they played together, and Karim felt happy, knowing he had found new friends. The next day, Samir's mother packed extra food for him to share. At school, Samir and Amir joined Karim again, sharing the extra food. Karim beamed, saying, "You and Amir are the best friends anyone could ask for."

As days passed, more students began sharing their lunches with those who had none. The school became a kinder, more generous place. One day, their teacher, Ms. Leila, praised the class, saying, "I am proud of you all for showing such kindness and generosity."

Samir felt proud too, knowing that sharing could make a big difference. He knew he would always remember this lesson.

Moral of the Story:

Always share with those in need. Generosity brings happiness to others and makes the world a better place.

Hadith:

The Prophet Muhammad (Sallallahu Alayhi Wasallam) said: "He is not a believer whose stomach is filled while the neighbor to his side goes hungry." (Sahih Bukhari, Hadith 112)

Chapter 5

The Patient Farmer

Once upon a time, in a small village called Sabir, there lived a farmer named Ahmad and his young son, Omar. Together, they worked on their farm, growing crops and taking care of animals. Omar loved helping his father, but he often grew impatient, wanting to see the results of their hard work immediately.

One sunny morning, Ahmad and Omar were planting seeds in their field. Omar looked at the tiny seeds in his hand and asked, "Father, when will these seeds grow into big plants?"

Ahmad smiled. "It takes time, Omar. We must be patient and take good care of them."

They finished planting the seeds, and Ahmad taught Omar how to water them gently. "We need to water the seeds every day," he explained. "The water will help them grow strong roots."

Every day, they watered the seeds, but Omar grew frustrated when he saw no signs of growth. "Father, why aren't the seeds growing?" he asked.

Ahmad replied, "Omar, the seeds are growing under the ground, where we can't see them yet. They need time to develop strong roots."

Omar tried to be patient, but it was hard. Seeing his son's impatience, Ahmad decided to teach him a lesson.

One evening, Ahmad took Omar for a walk to a large tree at the edge of their field. "Do you see this tree, Omar?" he asked. "It started as a tiny seed, just like ours. It took years to grow this big and strong. The tree had to be patient, just like we must be with our seeds."

Omar realized that good things take time and decided to be more patient. Days turned into weeks, and weeks into months. One morning, Omar saw tiny green sprouts poking through the soil. "Father, look! The seeds are growing!" he shouted with joy.

Ahmad smiled. "Yes, Omar, our patience and hard work are paying off."

Omar felt proud and continued caring for the plants with his father. They watered them, pulled out weeds, and ensured they got enough sunlight. As days passed, the plants grew taller and began to produce vegetables and fruits.

"Father, our plants are so big and healthy!" Omar said.

Ahmad nodded. "This is the result of patience and care. Good things come to those who wait and work hard."

Omar learned the value of patience and saw it lead to success. When they harvested their crops, Omar felt proud, understanding that patience was key. From that day on, he applied patience to everything he did, knowing it would always lead to good results.

Moral of the Story:

Be patient and work hard. Patience leads to success and helps us achieve our goals.

Hadith:

The Prophet Muhammad (Sallallahu Alayhi Wasallam) said: "The upper hand is better than the lower hand. The upper hand is that which gives, and the lower is that which receives. Start giving first to your dependents. The best objects of charity are those which are hanging in your hands and which are sufficient for your needs. Keep your tongue busy with remembering Allah, and keep your hand busy with giving charity." (Sahih Bukhari, Hadith 1427)

Chapter 6

The Compassionate Brother

Once upon a time, in a small village called Mehrab, there lived a kind little girl named Zainab and her younger brother, Hasan. They were very close, playing together, sharing stories, and helping each other with chores.

One day, Hasan became very sick with a high fever. Zainab was worried about her brother. Their mother, Fatima, took care of Hasan day and night, giving him medicine and keeping him comfortable. Zainab wanted to help too.

"Mother, can I help take care of Hasan?" Zainab asked. Fatima nodded. "Yes, Zainab. Be gentle and kind. Make sure he gets rest and feels loved."

Feeling happy to help, Zainab sat by Hasan's bed. "How are you feeling, Hasan?" she asked softly.

"I feel very tired, Zainab," Hasan whispered.

Zainab touched his forehead and felt its warmth. Remembering how Hasan loved stories, she asked, "Would you like me to tell you a story?"

Hasan nodded weakly, and Zainab began telling a story about a brave knight saving a village from a dragon. As she spoke, Hasan's eyes slowly closed, and he drifted off to sleep. Quietly, Zainab went to the kitchen and had an idea.

"Mother, can I make honey water for Hasan? It might make him feel better," she asked.

Fatima smiled proudly. "That's a wonderful idea, Zainab. Honey water can soothe his throat and give him strength."

Zainab carefully prepared the honey water and brought it to Hasan. "I made this for you," she said gently. Hasan took a sip and smiled weakly. "Thank you, Zainab. It's very nice."

Every day, Zainab did her best to care for Hasan, telling him stories and making sure he was comfortable. She helped with chores and brought Hasan water and medicine.

One morning, Zainab noticed that Hasan's fever had gone down. "How are you feeling today?" she asked.

Hasan smiled. "I feel a bit better, Zainab. Thank you for taking care of me."

"I'm so glad you're feeling better," Zainab said. "Keep resting to get strong again."

Days passed, and Hasan's health continued to improve. Zainab never stopped caring for him, and their bond grew even stronger.

Finally, the day came when Hasan was well again. He got out of bed, and they played together like before. "Thank you for taking care of me," Hasan said with a big smile. "You're the best sister."

Zainab hugged him tightly. "And you're the best brother. I'll always be here for you."

From then on, Zainab and Hasan knew they could count on each other. They learned the importance of compassion and caring for family.

Moral of the Story:

Be kind and take care of your family. When we help each other, we all feel happy and loved.

Hadith:

The Prophet Muhammad (Sallallahu Alayhi Wasallam) said: "The best among you are those who are best to their families." (Tirmidhi, Hadith 3895)

Chapter 7

The Brave Boy

THE BRAVE BOY

Once upon a time, in a village called Dosti, there lived a kind boy named Yaseen. He loved school and playing with his friends. However, a boy named Bilal at school often bullied others, taking their lunch or making fun of them because he was bigger and stronger.

One morning, Yaseen and his best friend Hamza heard someone crying on their way to school. They found a little boy named Ali sitting on the ground, with Bilal standing over him, holding his lunchbox.

"Give it back, Bilal!" Ali cried. "That's my lunch!"

Bilal laughed. "No, it's mine now," he said.

Yaseen knew it was wrong. He whispered to Hamza, "We have to do something."

Hamza, scared, replied, "No, Yaseen. Bilal is too strong."

Yaseen took a deep breath. "I'll do it," he decided. He approached Bilal and said firmly, "Bilal, give Ali his lunchbox back."

Bilal looked surprised. "What did you say?" he asked.

"I said give it back," Yaseen repeated. "It's wrong to take things that aren't yours."

Bilal's face turned red. "Do you want to fight me too?" he shouted.

Though nervous, Yaseen stood his ground. "I'm not afraid of you, Bilal. You need to stop."

A crowd of kids gathered around, watching. Bilal saw everyone staring at him and felt challenged. For a moment, it seemed he might hit Yaseen. But then he looked at Ali, still crying, and back at Yaseen, who stood firm.

"Fine," Bilal muttered, throwing the lunchbox down. "Take it. I don't want it anyway."

Yaseen picked up the lunchbox and handed it to Ali. "Here you go, Ali," he said with a smile.

Ali smiled back, "Thank you, Yaseen. You're very brave."

The other kids cheered for Yaseen, and even Hamza hugged him. Yaseen felt proud. From that day, he was known as the brave boy who stood up to the bully. Bilal stopped bullying because he knew Yaseen and his friends would always stand up to him.

At home, Yaseen's mother hugged him and said, "I'm so proud of you. It takes courage to stand up for what's right."

His father added, "Remember to always do the right thing, even when it's hard."

The next day, Yaseen saw Bilal sitting alone, looking sad. Feeling compassion, Yaseen sat next to him and said, "Do you want to sit with us for lunch?"

Bilal, surprised, asked, "Really? After everything I did?"

Yaseen nodded. "Everyone deserves a second chance."

From then on, Bilal became friends with Yaseen, Hamza, and Ali. He learned to be kind, and the school became a happier place where everyone looked out for each other.

Moral of the Story:

Be brave and always be kind. When we stand up for each other, good things happen.

Hadith:

The Prophet Muhammad (Sallallahu Alayhi Wasallam) said: "The best jihad is a word of truth in front of a tyrannical ruler." (Sunan Ibn Majah, Hadith 4012)

Chapter 8

The Thankful Child

THE THANKFUL CHILD

Once upon a time, there was a little girl named Amina. She was seven years old and loved playing with her many dolls, a beautiful dollhouse, and colorful books. Although Amina was a happy child, she didn't always remember to say "thank you" for what she had.

One sunny morning, Amina's mother said, "Amina, we are going to visit the orphanage today. Would you like to come?" Amina nodded excitedly; she had never been to an orphanage before.

When they arrived, Amina saw many children playing happily, even though they had few toys. A kind lady named Mrs. Fatima greeted them. "Welcome to our orphanage, Amina," she said with a smile. "Would you like to meet the children?"

Amina agreed and followed Mrs. Fatima inside. She noticed that each child had only a small bed and a few old, worn-out toys, but they still played with joy. Amina met a girl named Leila, who invited her to play with a simple puzzle, missing some pieces. Amina saw how much fun Leila was having.

"Do you like it here?" Amina asked.

Leila smiled, "Yes, I have many friends, and we play every day. I'm happy with what I have."

Amina was surprised. She thought of her room full of toys and realized that Leila was happy with so little. During lunch, Amina noticed the children enjoying simple food, grateful for their meal. She remembered how she sometimes complained about her own food and decided to be more thankful.

After saying goodbye, Amina was quiet on the way home, thinking about everything she had seen. She went to her room, looked at her many toys, and felt a warm feeling in her heart. She decided to share her toys with the children at the orphanage.

"Mom, can we go back to the orphanage tomorrow?" Amina asked.

"Of course, Amina," her mother replied. "Why do you want to go back?"

"I want to share my toys with the children. They don't have many, and I have so many. I want to make them happy," Amina explained.

Her mother smiled proudly. "That's a wonderful idea, Amina."

The next day, Amina packed a big box with her favorite toys, dolls, books, and games. She felt happy knowing she could share her blessings with others. At the orphanage, the children were overjoyed and thanked Amina with big smiles and hugs. Amina felt a warm glow in her heart, realizing that sharing and being thankful made her feel good inside.

From then on, Amina was grateful for everything she had and always remembered to say "thank you." She visited the orphanage regularly, sharing more toys and books with her new friends. Amina learned that being thankful for the little things made her happier and that sharing her blessings was a wonderful way to show gratitude.

Moral of the Story:

Be thankful for what you have and share with others. Gratitude and kindness make us happy and bring joy to those around us.

Hadith:

The Prophet Muhammad (Sallallahu Alayhi Wasallam) said: "He who does not thank people, does not thank Allah." (Tirmidhi, Hadith 1954)

Chapter 9

The Respectful Student

Once upon a time, there was a young boy named Omar. He was seven years old and loved school, playing with his friends, and learning new things. However, Omar didn't always listen to his teacher, Mrs. Aisha. He would talk during lessons and sometimes not do his homework.

One day, Mrs. Aisha gave the class a special project about the importance of respect. "Respect is very important," she said. "We must respect our parents, friends, and teachers."

Omar didn't understand why respecting his teacher was so important; he thought joking around was more fun. That evening, his mother asked him about his day.

"How was school today, Omar?" she asked.

"Mrs. Aisha gave us a project about respect," Omar replied.

"Do you know why respect is important?" she asked.

Omar shook his head. "Not really."

His mother explained, "Respect shows we value others. When you respect your teacher, you value her hard work and the knowledge she shares with you."

Omar thought about this. The next day, he listened more carefully in class, didn't talk to his friends during lessons, and did his homework. Mrs. Aisha noticed the change and smiled.

One day, Mrs. Aisha told the class a story about a boy named Ahmed who didn't always listen to his teacher. But when Ahmed decided to respect his teacher and learn as much as he could, he realized how valuable knowledge was.

Omar realized he needed to respect his teacher, just like Ahmed, and decided to be a better student. He started raising his hand before speaking and always said "please" and "thank you" to Mrs. Aisha. He did his homework on time and tried his best on every project. Mrs. Aisha was pleased with Omar's progress.

One afternoon, Mrs. Aisha shared a special Hadith: "The Prophet Muhammad (Sallallahu Alayhi Wasallam) said, 'Allah, His angels, and all those in the heavens and the earth pray for those who teach people good.' (Tirmidhi 2685)." Omar felt proud to learn and understood that respecting his teacher was part of seeking knowledge.

That evening, he asked his parents more about the Hadith. His father explained, "Teaching people good means sharing knowledge and respecting those who help you learn."

Omar decided to learn as much as he could and always respect his teachers. The next day, he continued to be respectful, and soon his friends followed his example. The whole class became more respectful.

One day, Mrs. Aisha gave Omar a special book. "I'm very proud of you, Omar," she said. "You have become a respectful student and are always eager to learn."

Omar felt proud and knew he had made the right choice by respecting his teacher. From that day on, he always tried his best to be a good student.

Moral of the Story:

Respect your teachers and always be eager to learn. Respect and knowledge go hand in hand.

Hadith:

The Prophet Muhammad (Sallallahu Alayhi Wasallam) said: "Allah, His angels, and all those in the heavens and the earth, even the ants in their hills and the fish in the sea, pray for those who teach people good." (Tirmidhi, Hadith 2685)

Chapter 10

The Polite Visitor

Once upon a time, there was a little boy named Ali, who was six years old and loved playing with his friends. One afternoon, his friend Hassan invited him to visit his house. Ali was excited because he had never been there before.

Before Ali left, his mother reminded him, "Remember to use good manners."

Ali asked, "What are good manners, Mom?"

She replied, "Good manners mean being polite and respectful. Say 'please' and 'thank you,' listen to Hassan's parents, and be kind."

Ali promised to remember and walked to Hassan's house down the street.

When he arrived, Hassan greeted him warmly. "Hi, Ali! I'm glad you came. Come meet my family."

Ali met Hassan's parents and said, "Hello, Mr. and Mrs. Hassan. Thank you for inviting me."

They smiled and welcomed him. "We're happy to have you, Ali."

Ali and Hassan played in Hassan's room, sharing toys and taking turns. Ali asked, "May I play with this toy, please?" Hassan agreed, and they had fun.

Later, Hassan's mother called them to the kitchen. "Boys, it's time for a snack." Ali and Hassan washed their hands and sat at the table. Mrs. Hassan served cookies and milk, and Ali said, "Thank you, Mrs. Hassan. These cookies look delicious."

"You're welcome, Ali. Enjoy!" she replied.

Hassan's little sister, Sara, joined them, and Ali invited her to play. "Hi, Sara. Would you like to play with us?" he asked. Sara nodded happily, and they built a big tower with blocks, sharing as they played.

When Hassan's father came home, Ali greeted him, "Hello, Mr. Hassan. It's nice to meet you."

Mr. Hassan smiled. "Hello, Ali. I'm glad you're here. You're a polite guest."

The boys played outside, and Ali admired the beautiful garden. "You have a lovely garden, Mr. Hassan," he said. Mr. Hassan thanked him and showed the boys the flowers and plants.

When it was time to go home, Ali thanked Hassan and his family. "Thank you for having me. I had a great time," he said.

"You're always welcome, Ali," Hassan's mother replied.

Back home, Ali's mother asked, "How was your visit?"

"It was wonderful, Mom. I used my good manners," Ali said proudly.

His mother hugged him. "I'm proud of you, Ali. Good manners are important."

From that day on, Ali always remembered to be polite and respectful, knowing it made him a better friend and guest.

Moral of the Story:

Be polite and respectful when visiting others. Good manners make everyone happy and help you make new friends.

Hadith:

The Prophet Muhammad (Sallallahu Alayhi Wasallam) said: "The best among you are those who have the best manners and character." (Sahih Bukhari, Hadith 3559)

Chapter 11

The Truthful Girl

Once upon a time, in a village called Sadiq, there lived a young girl named Aisha. Aisha was known for her kind heart and cheerful smile. She loved playing with her friends and helping her family. Her parents, Mr. and Mrs. Rahman, always taught her the importance of honesty.

One sunny afternoon, Aisha was playing with her favorite ball in the living room. She accidentally kicked the ball too hard, and it hit a vase on a shelf. The vase wobbled and crashed to the floor, breaking into many pieces.

Aisha's heart sank. She knew the vase was special to her mother, a gift from her grandmother. She felt tears in her eyes and thought about hiding the broken pieces, but she remembered what her parents always said: "Honesty is the best policy." Aisha knew she had to tell the truth.

Taking a deep breath, she went to the kitchen where her mother was cooking. "Mama, I need to tell you something," Aisha said softly.

Mrs. Rahman saw the worry on Aisha's face. "What is it, dear?" she asked.

Aisha's voice trembled. "I was playing in the living room, and I accidentally broke the vase. I'm really sorry, Mama."

Mrs. Rahman's face softened, and she hugged Aisha tightly. "Thank you for telling me the truth, Aisha. I know it wasn't easy, but I'm proud of you for being honest."

Aisha felt relieved. "I'm sorry, Mama. I didn't mean to break it."

"I know, Aisha," her mother said gently. "Accidents happen, but what's important is that you told the truth. We can replace things, but trust is very special."

Together, they cleaned up the broken pieces. Aisha felt grateful for her mother's understanding. She realized that telling the truth, even when it's hard, is the right thing to do.

The next day at school, Aisha shared her story with her best friend, Leila. "That was brave of you," Leila said. "I don't know if I could have done the same."

Aisha smiled. "It was scary, but honesty is always best."

Later, their teacher, Ms. Noor, asked the class to write about a time they had to be honest. Aisha shared her story, and Ms. Noor praised her for her courage. The class clapped, and Aisha felt proud.

As weeks passed, Aisha continued to be honest in her daily life, and her friends and family trusted her more. One evening, her father said, "I'm very proud of you, Aisha, for telling the truth about the vase. Honesty builds trust and respect."

Aisha promised to always be honest, knowing it made her feel good inside and helped her become a better person.

Moral of the Story:

Always tell the truth. Honesty builds trust and makes you feel good inside.

Hadith:

The Prophet Muhammad (Sallallahu Alayhi Wasallam) said: "Truthfulness leads to righteousness, and righteousness leads to Paradise. A man continues to tell the truth until he is recorded with Allah as a truthful person. Falsehood leads to wickedness, and wickedness leads to the Hellfire, and a man may continue to tell lies until he is recorded with Allah as a liar." (Sahih Muslim, Hadith 2607)

Chapter 12

The Forgiving Friend

THE FORGIVING FRIEND

Once upon a time, in a village called Dosti, there lived two best friends named Sarah and Layla. They did everything together — played games, did homework, and helped with chores. They loved each other like sisters.

One sunny afternoon, while playing in the park, they both wanted to go on the same swing. "I want to go first!" Sarah said. "No, I want to go first!" Layla replied. They began pulling the swing back and forth. Sarah accidentally pushed Layla, causing her to fall. Layla, upset, cried, "You pushed me!"

Sarah felt bad but was also angry. "Well, you were being mean!" she shouted. Layla ran home, not wanting to talk to Sarah. Sarah felt sad and didn't know what to do.

That evening, Sarah's mother noticed she was upset. "What's wrong, Sarah?" she asked. Sarah explained about the argument. Her mother hugged her and said, "Sometimes we say or do things we don't mean. The important thing is to apologize and ask for forgiveness. True friends forgive each other."

The next morning, Sarah went to Layla's house, feeling nervous. When Layla opened the door, Sarah said, "I'm really sorry for pushing you. I didn't mean to hurt you. Can you forgive me?"

Layla, remembering their fun times together, realized she missed her friend. "I'm sorry too, Sarah. I shouldn't have been so angry. I forgive you."

Sarah smiled and hugged Layla. "Thank you, Layla. You're my best friend, and I don't want to lose you."

Layla smiled back. "You're my best friend too. Let's never fight again."

They returned to the park, playing and laughing as they always did. They felt happy and grateful for each other's forgiveness. They made a promise to always talk about their problems instead of getting angry, taking deep breaths, and speaking kindly.

One day, their teacher, Mrs. Khan, noticed how well they were getting along. "You two are such good friends. What's your secret?"

"We forgive each other and let go of our anger," Layla replied.

Mrs. Khan nodded. "That's an important lesson. Forgiveness helps us stay close to the people we love."

Later, they saw their friend Amina looking sad. She explained she had a fight with a friend. Sarah and Layla encouraged her to apologize and make up, just as they had done.

Amina followed their advice and soon reconciled with her friend. Sarah and Layla felt happy knowing they had helped her.

From that day on, they continued practicing forgiveness, understanding that it made their friendship stronger. They promised always to forgive each other, knowing it made their bond unbreakable.

Moral of the Story:

Always forgive your friends. Forgiveness helps us stay happy and keeps our friendships strong.

Hadith:

The Prophet Muhammad (Sallallahu Alayhi Wasallam) said: "The strong person is not the one who can overpower others. Rather, the strong person is the one who can control himself when he gets angry." (Sahih Bukhari, Hadith 6114)

Chapter 13

The Fair Judge

In a little town called Harmonia, there was a bright school named Al-Farooq Elementary. The children loved to learn and play together. Every year, the school held a special event called the School Play Day.

This year, the play was about justice, titled "The Fair Judge." The teachers chose a kind boy named Ahmed to play the role of the wise judge. Ahmed was excited but nervous and practiced his lines daily with his friends. Ali played a shopkeeper, Fatima a farmer, and other children played villagers and animals. Everyone was excited.

On the day of the play, the school hall filled with parents, teachers, and students. The stage was decorated, and the play began. Ahmed, as the judge, listened carefully to each case brought before him.

The first case was between Ali the shopkeeper and Fatima the farmer. Fatima complained, "Judge Ahmed, Ali took my apples without asking."

Ali explained, "I was hungry and didn't have money to buy food."

Ahmed thought carefully and said, "Ali, it is wrong to take something without permission. You must apologize to Fatima and return the apples or pay for them. Fatima, please share some apples with Ali."

Ali apologized, and Fatima shared her apples. The audience clapped for the fair decision.

The next case was about two boys, Bilal and Omar, arguing over a lost soccer ball. Bilal said, "Omar lost my soccer ball. I let him borrow it, but now he can't find it."

Omar explained, "I didn't mean to lose it. It rolled away, and I couldn't find it."

Ahmed decided, "Omar should help Bilal look for the ball. If they can't find it, Omar should give Bilal a new soccer ball." The boys agreed, shook hands, and the audience cheered.

The last case was about Aisha and her missing pet cat, Mittens. Ahmed suggested they ask the villagers if anyone had seen Mittens. The children and villagers searched together. A kind old man said, "I saw a cat near the bakery."

They rushed to the bakery and found Mittens hiding. Aisha hugged her pet, and the villagers cheered.

Ahmed smiled and said, "Justice is about fairness, kindness, and helping each other."

The play ended with a big round of applause. The children felt proud of their performance, and Ahmed was happy he had learned to be a fair judge. As the audience left, they remembered the lesson that being fair and kind made their community better.

Moral of the Story:

Always be fair and kind. Helping others and making fair decisions is important.

Hadith:

The Prophet Muhammad (Sallallahu Alayhi Wasallam) said: "Allah loves those who are just." (Sahih Muslim, Hadith 1827)

Chapter 14

The Loving Parent

THE LOVING PARENT

In a cozy village named Salaam, lived a kind mother named Amina and her little daughter, Noor. They lived in a small house with a beautiful garden full of flowers. Every morning, the sun would shine brightly, and the birds would sing sweet songs.

Amina loved Noor very much. She made sure Noor had healthy food, clean clothes, and a safe place to sleep. Noor loved her mother, knowing how hard she worked to make her happy.

One sunny morning, Noor woke up with a big smile and ran to her mother. "Good morning, Mama!" she said.

Amina smiled back, "Good morning, my sweet Noor! How did you sleep?"

"I slept well, Mama. Can we go to the garden and play today?" Noor asked.

"Of course, my dear. But first, let's have breakfast," Amina replied.

Amina made a delicious breakfast of bread, honey, and fresh milk. They sat together and enjoyed their meal, believing that sharing meals brought them closer.

After breakfast, they went to the garden. Noor loved playing among the flowers, running around and laughing. Amina watched her with a loving smile, happy to see her daughter so joyful.

One day, Noor was playing in the park when she fell and hurt her knee. She cried out in pain. Amina heard her and ran to her side, hugging her. "It's okay, my dear. Mama is here."

Amina gently cleaned Noor's knee, put a bandage on it, and said, "You are very brave, my sweet Noor. The pain will go away soon."

Noor smiled and said, "Thank you, Mama. You always make me feel better."

Amina hugged Noor tightly, knowing her love was the most important thing she could give her daughter. As Noor grew older, she remembered how her mother always took care of her and wanted to be just like her.

One evening, Amina told Noor a bedtime story about a lost bird and its mother who searched everywhere to find her baby and keep it safe. "Just like the mother bird, I will always take care of you, Noor," Amina said.

Noor hugged her mother and said, "I love you, Mama. You are the best mother in the world."

Every day, Amina showed Noor how much she loved her, ensuring she was happy and safe. Noor learned to be kind and caring to everyone, understanding that her mother's love was special. From that day on, Noor remembered her mother's words and always tried to be kind and caring, knowing her mother's love had taught her the most important lesson of all.

Moral of the Story:

Always show love and care. It makes our hearts happy and our lives beautiful.

Hadith:

The Prophet Muhammad (Sallallahu Alayhi Wasallam) said: "Allah is merciful only to those who show mercy to others." (Sahih Bukhari, Hadith 5997)

Chapter 15

The Curious Learner

In a peaceful village named Ilm, there lived a curious boy named Hasan. He loved asking questions and learning new things. His parents, Fatima and Ali, encouraged his curiosity and always helped him find answers.

One morning, Hasan asked his mother, "Why is the sky blue?"

Fatima smiled. "The sky looks blue because of how sunlight interacts with our atmosphere. Blue light scatters the most, which is why we see the sky as blue."

"Wow, that's amazing!" Hasan replied.

Later, Hasan saw a butterfly in the garden and asked his father, "Why do butterflies have colorful wings?"

Ali explained, "Butterflies have colorful wings to attract mates and warn predators. The colors help them survive in nature."

"I love learning new things!" Hasan exclaimed with excitement.

One day, Hasan's teacher, Mrs. Khan, announced a science fair at school. The children could choose any topic to present. Hasan decided to learn about how plants grow and shared his idea with his parents, who were very supportive.

"We will help you, Hasan," said Fatima. "Let's start by planting some seeds in the garden."

Hasan and his parents planted flowers, vegetables, and herbs. He watered them daily and kept a journal of his observations. One morning, he saw tiny green shoots emerging from the soil.

"Mama, Baba, come look! The seeds are growing!" Hasan shouted excitedly.

Fatima and Ali smiled proudly. "You are doing a great job," said Ali.

As the plants grew, Hasan noticed some grew faster than others. He asked his mother, "Why do some plants grow faster?"

Fatima explained, "Different plants need different amounts of sunlight, water, and nutrients. Each plant is unique, just like people."

Hasan wrote down everything he learned and drew pictures of the plants at different stages of growth. On the day of the science fair, he proudly presented his project with pictures and notes about plant growth. He also brought the plants he had grown in the garden.

His friend Amina said, "Wow, Hasan, this is amazing! I didn't know so much about plants."

Mrs. Khan added, "You did a wonderful job, Hasan. Keep asking questions and seeking knowledge."

Hasan felt proud and happy. As they walked home, Ali said, "We are so proud of you. Seeking knowledge is very important."

Fatima added, "Our Prophet Muhammad (Sallallahu Alayhi Wasallam) encouraged us to always seek knowledge."

Hasan smiled, "I will always keep learning, Mama and Baba."

That evening, Hasan felt grateful for his parents and his teacher. He knew that seeking knowledge would help him grow and become a better person.

Moral of the Story:

Always be curious and seek knowledge. Learning new things helps us understand the world better and makes us wiser.

Hadith:

The Prophet Muhammad (Sallallahu Alayhi Wasallam) said: "Seeking knowledge is an obligation upon every Muslim." (Sunan Ibn Majah, Hadith 224)

Chapter 16

The Humble Leader

At Harmony Elementary, there was a smart and kind boy named Yusuf, loved by everyone for being helpful and friendly. One day, the principal, Mrs. Rahim, announced they would choose a new school captain to lead the students and improve the school.

Many students, including Yusuf, wanted to be the school captain. On the election day, Yusuf gave his speech:

"Good morning, everyone. I want to be the school captain to help all of you. A leader should be kind and humble. If chosen, I will listen to everyone and work hard to make our school a great place."

The students clapped for Yusuf, and when the votes were counted, Mrs. Rahim announced, "The new school captain is Yusuf!" Yusuf was happy and promised to be a good leader.

The next day, Yusuf began his new role. He walked around the school, talking to students and teachers, listening to their ideas, and helping with their problems. One day, a little girl named Aisha told him the playground was crowded, and they needed more swings.

Yusuf went to Mrs. Rahim and explained the issue. She agreed and worked with him to get new swings for the playground. The students were very happy and thanked Yusuf for his help.

During a school assembly, Yusuf noticed some students were not listening. He gently reminded them, "It's important to pay attention and show respect to our teachers. Let's all try to listen better next time." The students agreed and promised to listen more carefully.

Yusuf also organized a cleanup day at the school, asking all the students to help clean the school yard and classrooms. Everyone worked together, and Yusuf showed that a true leader helps others and works with them.

One day, a boy named Bilal asked Yusuf for help with his math homework. Yusuf sat with Bilal and helped him understand the problems, making Bilal very grateful.

Yusuf continued to lead with kindness and humility, always listening and helping his friends. He knew being a leader was about serving others and making them feel valued.

One day, Mrs. Rahim told Yusuf, "You have been a wonderful school captain. You lead with humility and kindness. You are a true example of a good leader."

Yusuf felt happy and proud. His friends appreciated him, knowing he cared about them and always did his best for everyone. Yusuf's leadership made the school a happier and better place.

Moral of the Story:

A true leader is kind and humble. Leading with humility means serving others and making them feel valued.

Hadith:

The Prophet Muhammad (Sallallahu Alayhi Wasallam) said: "The leader of a people is their servant." (Sahih Bukhari, Hadith 2551)

Chapter 17

The Gentle Shepherd

In a small village named Rahma, there lived a kind shepherd boy named Sami. At twelve years old, Sami loved taking care of his family's flock of sheep. Every morning, he would wake up early, gather the sheep, and lead them to the green pastures near the hills.

Sami knew each of his sheep by name and made sure they were always safe and happy. His father, Omar, had taught him to be gentle and kind to animals.

One sunny morning, as Sami was leading the sheep to the pasture, he noticed a little lamb named Lulu limping. Sami quickly checked Lulu's hoof and found a small thorn.

"Oh no, Lulu! Let me help you," Sami said softly. He carefully removed the thorn and comforted Lulu, who bleated softly in thanks. Sami smiled and patted her head. He remembered how Prophet Muhammad (peace be upon him) always showed kindness to animals and wanted to follow his example.

At the pasture, Sami let the sheep graze on the fresh grass while he sat under a tree with his book about animals. Suddenly, he heard a loud bleating. Sami saw that a big ram named Rafi was stuck in a bush, struggling to free himself.

Sami quickly ran over and said, "Don't worry, Rafi. I'm here to help you." He carefully untangled Rafi from the bush. Rafi nuzzled Sami's hand in thanks, and Sami gently patted his head. "Be careful next time, Rafi," he said.

Throughout the day, Sami made sure his sheep were well-fed, had enough water, and were safe in the shade. He knew taking care of the sheep was a big responsibility, but he loved doing it.

In the evening, Sami led the sheep back home. The sky was painted with beautiful colors as the sun set, and Sami felt peaceful, knowing he had done a good job.

When they reached home, Sami's father, Omar, greeted them with a smile. "Welcome back, Sami. How was your day with the sheep?"

"It was good, Baba. I took care of Lulu's thorn and helped Rafi get out of a bush. I made sure they were all safe and happy," Sami replied.

Omar patted Sami on the back and said, "I'm proud of you, Sami. You are a kind and gentle shepherd. Always remember to show kindness to all animals, as our Prophet Muhammad (peace be upon him) taught us."

That night, Sami felt happy knowing he had taken good care of his sheep. He knew that being kind to animals was a way to show love and respect for all of Allah's creations.

Moral of the Story:

Always be kind to animals. Taking care of them with love and gentleness is very important.

Hadith:

The Prophet Muhammad (Sallallahu Alayhi Wasallam) said: "Whoever is kind to the creatures of God is kind to himself." (Sunan Abu Dawood, Hadith 2550)

Chapter 18

The Responsible Child

In a small town called Amanah, there lived a cheerful little girl named Hana. Hana loved playing with her toys, especially her favorite teddy bear, Tuffy, a gift from her grandmother. She took Tuffy everywhere she went.

One sunny afternoon, Hana and her best friend, Sara, went to the park. They played on the swings and slides, and Hana hugged Tuffy tightly. When they decided to play hide and seek, Hana placed Tuffy on a bench, saying, "Stay here, Tuffy. I'll be right back," and ran off to hide.

After playing, Hana ran home excitedly but soon realized, "Oh no! I left Tuffy at the park!"

Hana's mother, Maryam, saw how upset she was and said, "Don't worry, Hana. Let's go back to the park and find Tuffy."

They hurried back to the park, but Tuffy was gone. Hana cried, "Mama, Tuffy is gone. What if I never find him again?"

Maryam hugged her and said, "This is a good time to learn a lesson about being responsible. Let's look around and ask if anyone has seen Tuffy."

They searched the park and asked people, but Tuffy was nowhere to be found. Hana felt sad and guilty for not taking care of her toy.

That evening, Maryam sat beside Hana in her room and said, "Taking care of our belongings shows we are responsible. We should always know where our things are and bring them back home."

The next day at school, Hana felt sad. Her teacher, Mrs. Khan, noticed and asked, "Hana, is everything okay?"

Hana explained about losing Tuffy. Mrs. Khan said, "Losing something special is hard, but it's also a chance to learn. We all make mistakes; it's important to learn from them."

Hana nodded and said, "I want to be more responsible."

After school, Hana went to the park, hoping to find Tuffy. Just as she was about to give up, a kind lady approached and said, "Are you looking for a teddy bear? I found one on the bench yesterday."

Hana's eyes lit up with hope. "Yes! That's my Tuffy! Thank you so much!"

The lady returned Tuffy, and Hana hugged her teddy bear tightly. On the way home, Hana promised to always take care of her belongings.

Maryam said, "I'm proud of you, Hana. You learned an important lesson about responsibility."

Hana smiled, "I promise to be more responsible from now on, Mama."

Moral of the Story:

Always take care of your belongings. Being responsible helps us keep our things safe and shows that we value them.

Hadith:

The Prophet Muhammad (Sallallahu Alayhi Wasallam) said: "The strong believer is better and more beloved to Allah than the weak believer, while there is good in both. Strive for that which will benefit you, seek the help of Allah, and do not feel helpless." (Sahih Muslim, Hadith 2664)

Chapter 19

The Faithful Believer

Once upon a time, in a peaceful village, lived a little girl named Sara. She was seven years old with bright eyes and a smile that could light up a room. She loved playing with her friends, reading books, and spending time with her family. Her family taught her about Allah and the importance of trusting Him in both good and bad times.

One sunny morning, Sara woke up excited for the village fair. She had been waiting for weeks, eager to ride the big Ferris wheel. At the fair, Sara's eyes sparkled with joy at the colorful balloons, laughter, and the smell of popcorn. Holding her mother's hand, she felt safe and happy.

After playing games and winning a small stuffed bear, Sara saw the Ferris wheel. "I want to ride it!" she begged. Her father agreed, and they got in line. Soon, they climbed into the big seat, and the Ferris wheel began moving. As it went higher, Sara saw the whole fair below, looking tiny from above.

But suddenly, the Ferris wheel stopped at the top. Sara felt scared. "Why did it stop, Daddy?" she asked.

Her father squeezed her hand and said, "Sometimes things happen, but we must trust in Allah. We're safe up here." He told her stories about how Allah always takes care of us, like the story of Prophet

Ibrahim (Alayhis Salaam), who trusted Allah when he was thrown into the fire, and Allah protected him.

Sara felt comforted and whispered a small prayer, "Please, Allah, keep us safe." Soon, the Ferris wheel started moving again, and they came down slowly. Sara felt relieved and happy. Her mother hugged her tightly. "You were so brave, Sara!"

Sara smiled. "I was scared, but I trusted Allah."

Her parents beamed with pride. "Always remember to trust in Allah, even when things are tough."

Sara enjoyed the rest of the fair, feeling much braver. That night, she realized how important it was to have faith and trust in Allah. She felt grateful for her family and everything she had learned.

The next day at school, Sara shared her story with her friends, telling them about the Ferris wheel and how she learned to trust in Allah. Her friends shared their own stories, making Sara happy to know they all shared the same faith and trust.

From that day on, whenever Sara faced something scary or difficult, she remembered the Ferris wheel and her father's words. She knew Allah was always with her, protecting and guiding her.

Moral of the Story:

Always trust in Allah, even when things are difficult. Allah is always with us and will take care of us.

Hadith:

The Prophet Muhammad (Sallallahu Alayhi Wasallam) said: "Be mindful of Allah, and you will find Him in front of you. Recognize and acknowledge Allah in times of ease and prosperity, and He will remember you in times of adversity." (Tirmidhi, Hadith 2516)

Chapter 20

The Cheerful Helper

Once upon a time in a small village, there lived a boy named Ali. Ali was eight years old, with a kind heart and a big smile. He loved helping his family and friends and learning new ways to help others.

One day, Ali heard about a special community event where people would come together to help those in need. Ali's mother told him they could volunteer to help. Ali was excited and asked, "What will we do, Mama?"

"We will help serve food and clean up afterward," his mother explained.

On the day of the event, Ali and his mother arrived early. They helped set up tables and prepare the area. Ali put on an apron and went to the kitchen to help serve food. His job was to scoop food onto plates and hand them to people in line. He greeted everyone with a big smile, saying, "Enjoy your meal!"

As he worked, Ali noticed an old man who looked very tired. The man smiled at Ali and said, "Thank you, young man. Your smile makes my day better." Ali felt happy, realizing that even a small act of kindness could brighten someone's day.

Later, Ali saw some children who seemed shy to join the games. He walked over and invited them, "Do you want to play with us? We have lots of games!" The children smiled, joined in, and had a wonderful time. Ali felt joyful seeing everyone so happy.

At the end of the day, Ali and his mother helped clean up. They picked up trash and washed dishes. Ali was tired but very happy. On the way home, his mother said, "I'm proud of you, Ali. You worked hard and helped so many people."

Ali smiled and replied, "I feel happy, Mama. It was fun to help others and see them smile."

His mother nodded. "That's the joy of helping others. The Prophet Muhammad (Sallallahu Alayhi Wasallam) taught us to help those in need."

Ali thought about what his mother said and felt even happier. He decided to help others every chance he got. The next day at school, he shared his experience, inspiring his friends to help at the next event.

From that day on, Ali looked for ways to help people, whether by carrying groceries, picking up litter, or helping his teacher. He realized that even small acts of kindness made a difference.

Ali's heart was full of joy every time he helped someone, remembering the lesson his mother taught him.

Moral of the Story:

Helping others brings joy to our hearts and makes the world a better place.

Hadith:

The Prophet Muhammad (Sallallahu Alayhi Wasallam) said: "Whoever relieves a believer's distress of the distressful aspects of this world, Allah will rescue him from a difficulty of the difficulties of the Hereafter." (Sahih Muslim, Hadith 2699)

Chapter 21

The Sincere Worshipper

Once upon a time in a small village, there lived a boy named Ahmed. He was seven years old, with a big heart and a curious mind. Ahmed loved playing with his friends, reading books, and spending time with his family. His family taught him the importance of prayer, known as Salah, as a way to talk to Allah.

One day, Ahmed's father called him, "Ahmed, it's time for Salah. Let's go to the mosque together." Ahmed liked going to the mosque with his father and enjoyed the peaceful feeling of praying there.

At the mosque, Ahmed learned how to do Wudu, the special washing before prayer. As they prayed, Ahmed tried to follow along, but sometimes his mind wandered to his toys and friends. After the prayer, his father gently reminded him, "When we pray, we should focus on Allah and talk to Him with our hearts."

Ahmed nodded but found it hard to understand. That evening, his grandmother visited. Ahmed asked her, "Grandma, can you tell me a story about prayer?"

She smiled warmly. "Of course, Ahmed. Let me tell you about a sincere worshipper named Omar."

Omar, like Ahmed, loved to play but loved praying to Allah even more. One day, when his village faced a drought, Omar joined the villagers to pray for rain. He prayed with all his heart, trusting that Allah would listen. Soon, it began to rain! The villagers were overjoyed, knowing Omar's sincere prayer had been answered.

Ahmed listened with wide eyes. "Wow, Grandma! Omar's prayer was answered because he was sincere?"

"Yes, Ahmed," she replied. "When we pray sincerely, Allah listens. Salah is a special time to connect with Allah."

Inspired, Ahmed decided to pray with sincerity, like Omar. That night, he made a special prayer, talking to Allah with all his heart. The next morning, he felt happy and peaceful.

At breakfast, Ahmed shared, "Daddy, Grandma, I prayed with all my heart last night, and it felt so good!"

His father and grandmother smiled. "That's wonderful, Ahmed. Sincere prayer brings us closer to Allah and fills our hearts with peace."

Ahmed decided to make every prayer sincere and focused, knowing that Allah was always listening. From that day on, he prayed with all his heart, feeling a special connection with Allah and filling his heart with joy and peace.

Moral of the Story:

When we pray with sincerity and focus, Allah listens to us and fills our hearts with peace.

Hadith:

The Prophet Muhammad (Sallallahu Alayhi Wasallam) said: "The closest a person is to his Lord is when he is in prostration, so increase in supplication." (Sahih Muslim, Hadith 482)

Chapter 22

The Generous Host

THE GENEROUS HOST

Once upon a time in a small village, there lived a boy named Karim with his parents and younger sister, Layla. Their home was filled with love, and their parents always taught them to be kind and generous, especially to guests.

One day, Karim's father announced, "We are having special guests tomorrow from a nearby village." Karim and Layla were excited and helped prepare the house. They cleaned the living room, set up extra beds, and decorated with fresh flowers from the garden.

"We want our guests to feel special and welcomed," said their father. Karim's mother cooked delicious food, and the smell of freshly baked bread and warm stew filled the house. Karim and Layla set the table, ensuring everything was perfect.

When the guests arrived—a friendly couple with two children named Ali and Amina—Karim and Layla greeted them with big smiles. "Welcome to our home!" they said.

The guests felt at home right away. Karim and Layla showed Ali and Amina around the house and garden, and they played games together, having lots of fun.

At dinner, everyone gathered around the table, enjoying plates of delicious food and sharing stories. The house was filled with joy and laughter. After dinner, Karim's mother served a special dessert, baklava. "This is amazing!" Ali exclaimed, licking his fingers.

That night, Karim's father told them, "You both did a wonderful job today. Being a good host means making your guests feel welcome and happy. You showed kindness and generosity."

Karim felt proud. He realized how important it was to be a good host. The next morning, he woke up early to help prepare breakfast. When the guests came to the table, they were delighted to see the delicious spread waiting for them.

Throughout their stay, Karim and Layla continued to make their guests feel welcome, playing games, sharing toys, and showing them around the village.

On the day the guests were leaving, they helped them pack and felt a little sad to see them go. "Thank you for being such amazing hosts," said Ali's father.

Karim's father replied, "It was our pleasure. You are always welcome in our home."

That evening, Karim's father reminded them of the Prophet Muhammad's (Sallallahu Alayhi Wasallam) teaching: "Whoever believes in Allah and the Last Day, let him honor his guest." (Bukhari, Hadith 6136).

From that day on, Karim and Layla always remembered to welcome guests with kindness and generosity, knowing it was a beautiful way to show love and respect.

Moral of the Story:

Welcoming guests with kindness and generosity makes them feel special and loved.

Hadith:

The Prophet Muhammad (Sallallahu Alayhi Wasallam) said: "Whoever believes in Allah and the Last Day, let him honor his guest." (Sahih Bukhari, Hadith 6136)

Chapter 23

The Patient Mother

THE PATIENT MOTHER

Once upon a time, in a small village, there lived a boy named Yusuf. Yusuf was a curious and energetic child who loved exploring and asking questions. His mother, Fatima, loved him very much and always tried to be patient with him.

One morning, Yusuf asked excitedly, "Mama, can we go to the park today?"

Fatima smiled and agreed, "Of course, Yusuf. But first, we need to have breakfast and tidy up the house."

Yusuf quickly finished breakfast and tried to help clean, but accidentally knocked over a vase, spilling water and flowers everywhere.

Fatima took a deep breath and said, "It's okay, Yusuf. Accidents happen. Let's clean it up together." Yusuf was surprised his mother wasn't angry, and they cleaned up the mess together.

At the park, Yusuf played and got his clothes muddy from jumping in a puddle. Fatima gently reminded him, "Your clothes are dirty, but I see you're having fun. Just remember to be careful." Yusuf felt grateful for his mother's patience.

Back home, after a bath, Yusuf decided to draw a picture for his mother. As he moved, his crayons fell to the floor. Fatima calmly said, "Yusuf, it's important to keep things organized. Let's pick them up together." She showed him how to keep the crayons in a box so they wouldn't roll away.

While they ate lunch, Fatima told Yusuf a story about patience, saying, "Being patient helps us stay calm and solve problems." Yusuf listened and felt proud of his mother, wanting to be patient like her.

Later, when Yusuf's toy car got stuck under the sofa, he felt frustrated. Fatima showed him how to use a stick to gently push the car out. "See, Yusuf, when we are patient, we can find a solution," she said.

Yusuf hugged his mother. "Thank you, Mama. I'll try to be more patient like you."

That evening, Fatima shared a Hadith with him: "The strong person is not the one who can overpower others. Rather, the strong person is the one who controls himself when he gets angry." (Bukhari, Hadith 6114).

Yusuf felt proud to follow the teachings of the Prophet Muhammad (Sallallahu Alayhi Wasallam). "I'll always try to be patient, Mama," he promised.

From that day on, Yusuf practiced patience, remembering his mother's example and the teachings of the Prophet. He knew that being patient made him stronger and helped him solve problems calmly.

Moral of the Story:

Patience helps us stay calm and find solutions to problems.

Hadith:

The Prophet Muhammad (Sallallahu Alayhi Wasallam) said: "The strong person is not the one who can overpower others. Rather, the strong person is the one who controls himself when he gets angry." (Sahih Bukhari, Hadith 6114)

Chapter 24

The Grateful Son

Once upon a time, in a small village, there lived a cheerful and curious boy named Ali. He loved playing outside with his friends and exploring new things. Ali lived with his parents, Hassan and Layla, who loved him very much. Hassan was a hardworking farmer, and Layla took care of the house, cooked meals, and helped Ali with his schoolwork. Even though they were always busy, they made sure Ali had everything he needed.

One sunny morning, Ali woke up and smelled the delicious aroma of freshly baked bread and warm milk. "Good morning, Mama!" he said cheerfully. Layla smiled and replied, "Good morning, Ali. Come and have your breakfast." After breakfast, Ali ran outside to play with his friends. He played games, ran around, and had lots of fun.

When it was time for lunch, Ali returned home, feeling very hungry. As he entered the house, he saw his mother still working hard in the kitchen. She looked tired but kept going. Ali thought, "Mama is always working so hard for me. I should help her more." After lunch, Ali decided to help his mother clean the house. He picked up his toys, swept the floor, and even tried to wash the dishes. Layla was surprised and happy to see her son helping. "Thank you, Ali. You are such a good boy," she said, giving him a big hug.

Ali felt proud and happy. He realized that helping his parents made them happy and showed how much he appreciated their hard work. From that day on, he tried to help his parents every day.

One evening, after a long day of work, Hassan came home feeling very tired. He sat down on a chair and sighed. Ali noticed his father's tiredness and thought, "Baba works so hard in the fields every day. I should do something nice for him." Ali decided to draw a picture for his father. He drew a picture of their family: his father working in the fields, his mother cooking, and himself helping them. He colored the picture with bright colors and wrote, "Thank you, Baba and Mama, for everything you do for me. I love you."

When Hassan saw the picture, his eyes filled with tears of joy. He hugged Ali tightly and said, "Thank you, my dear son. This is the best gift I have ever received." Ali's heart was filled with happiness. He realized how important it was to thank his parents and show them love and appreciation.

Ali remembered a story his teacher had told him about respecting parents. She had shared a Hadith: "The Prophet Muhammad (Sallallahu Alayhi Wasallam) said, 'Heaven lies under the feet of your mother.'" Ali thought about this Hadith and understood its meaning. He knew it was important to respect and thank his parents.

From that day on, Ali made sure to help his mother with cooking and cleaning and his father in the fields whenever he could. His parents were proud of their son. They saw how kind and helpful he had become and were grateful for his love and care.

Moral of the Story:

It is important to thank and help our parents for all they do for us.

Hadith:

The Prophet Muhammad (Sallallahu Alayhi Wasallam) said: "Heaven lies under the feet of your mother." (Sunan an-Nasa'i, Hadith 3104)

Chapter 25

The Honest Worker

THE HONEST WORKER

Once upon a time in a small village, there was a young boy named Omar. Omar was kind, curious, and loved learning new things. He lived with his parents, who taught him to be honest and work hard.

One day, Omar's father said, "Omar, you are old enough to start learning a trade. I want you to work with Mr. Karim, the carpenter. He is a good man and will teach you many valuable skills."

Omar was excited to start his new job. The next morning, he went to Mr. Karim's workshop. Mr. Karim welcomed Omar warmly and said, "I am happy to have you as my apprentice. Together, we will make beautiful furniture."

Omar quickly learned that working with wood was not easy. He had to be patient and careful. Mr. Karim showed him how to measure the wood, cut it, and shape it into different items. Omar tried his best to do everything just like Mr. Karim.

One day, a customer came to the workshop and asked Mr. Karim to make a strong table. Mr. Karim chose the best wood and said, "Omar, always choose the best materials. This way, your customers will trust you." Omar nodded and helped Mr. Karim build the table. After several days, the table was ready. It was beautiful and strong, just like the customer wanted.

The customer was very happy and said, "Thank you, Mr. Karim, for your honest work." Mr. Karim replied, "I believe in doing honest work and using good materials."

Omar felt proud to learn from Mr. Karim. He understood that being honest and careful was important. One day, Omar noticed a small crack in a piece of wood for a chair. "Mr. Karim, there is a crack in this wood," he said.

Mr. Karim looked at the wood and said, "You are right, Omar. We cannot use this piece; it might break." He replaced the cracked wood, even though it meant more work. Omar realized that being honest sometimes meant doing extra work to make sure everything was right.

As the days passed, Omar saw how Mr. Karim treated all his customers with respect and honesty. One day, a woman brought a broken chair to the workshop. "Can you fix this chair for me?" she asked.

Mr. Karim said, "Yes, I will make it strong and safe." Omar watched as Mr. Karim carefully repaired the chair. When the woman returned, she was very pleased. "Thank you, Mr. Karim," she said. "You did a wonderful job."

One day, Omar made a small wooden box by himself. He was proud and showed it to Mr. Karim. Mr. Karim said, "You did a great job, but there is a small crack here. Always check your work carefully."

Omar felt a little sad, but Mr. Karim encouraged him. "Don't worry, Omar. This is how we learn. Always be honest and fix mistakes. You will become a skilled worker."

One evening, Mr. Karim told Omar, "The Prophet Muhammad (Sallallahu Alayhi Wasallam) taught us that being honest is very valuable. Always be honest and work with integrity."

Omar felt proud to follow the Prophet's teachings. He promised to always be honest and work hard, just like Mr. Karim.

Moral of the Story:

Always be honest and dedicated in your work.

Hadith:

The Prophet Muhammad (Sallallahu Alayhi Wasallam) said: "The truthful, honest merchant is with the Prophets, the truthful, and the martyrs." (Tirmidhi, Hadith 1209)

Chapter 26

The Gentle Friend

Once upon a time, in a peaceful village, there lived a cheerful young girl named Amina. She loved playing with her friends, running around, and exploring the fields near her home. Amina's parents, Farid and Maryam, taught her to always be kind and gentle with everyone.

One sunny morning, Amina woke up with a big smile. She was excited to go to school. After breakfast, she said, "Goodbye, Mama! Goodbye, Baba! I'm going to school!" Her mother replied, "Goodbye, Amina! Have a wonderful day and remember to be kind."

At school, Amina loved learning new things and playing with her best friend, Zara. They always had fun together. But there was one boy in their class, Omar, who often felt lonely and sad. He was shy and didn't have many friends.

One day during recess, Amina and Zara were playing a game when they noticed Omar sitting alone. Amina felt sorry for him and decided to invite him to play. She ran over and asked, "Hi Omar, would you like to play with us?" Omar smiled shyly and replied, "Okay, thank you."

Soon, Omar was laughing and having a great time with them. Amina felt happy to see Omar smiling. Later, in the classroom, their teacher, Mrs. Laila, asked the students to share a kind act they did. Amina raised her hand and shared how they invited Omar to play. "That's wonderful," said Mrs. Laila. "Kind words and actions make a big difference."

Amina felt proud and decided to always be kind to everyone. One afternoon, while working on a school project, Zara accidentally knocked over their model, breaking it into pieces. Zara looked upset, but Amina said gently, "It's okay, Zara. We can fix it together." Zara smiled with relief, and together, they made the model even better.

One day, after school, Amina saw her neighbor, Grandma Fatima, struggling to carry groceries. Amina ran over and said, "Let me help you, Grandma Fatima." Grandma Fatima thanked her warmly. As they walked, she shared stories about her youth, and Amina enjoyed listening.

A few days later, at the village market, Amina saw a little boy crying because he had lost his mother. She went up to him and said gently, "Don't worry. I'll help you find your mother." She took his hand and walked around the market until they found his mother, who thanked Amina for her kindness.

That evening, Amina's father, Farid, said, "Amina, I heard you helped a boy today. I am very proud of you." Amina smiled and replied, "I learned that being kind is very important."

Her father nodded and said, "The Prophet Muhammad (Sallallahu Alayhi Wasallam) taught us to speak kind words or stay silent. This means we should always be kind to others." Amina felt proud to follow the Prophet's teachings and promised to always be kind and help others.

Moral of the Story:

Always speak kindly to others and help those in need.

Hadith:

The Prophet Muhammad (Sallallahu Alayhi Wasallam) said: "Whoever believes in Allah and the Last Day should speak a good word or remain silent." (Sahih Bukhari, Hadith 6475)

Chapter 27

The Caring Nurse

Once upon a time, in a small village, there lived a little girl named Mariam. Mariam was kind and cheerful and loved spending time with her family. She lived with her parents and her dear Grandma Aisha.

One day, Grandma Aisha became very sick. She had a bad cough and felt very weak. Mariam's parents, Fatima and Ahmed, took her to the doctor. The doctor said, "Grandma Aisha needs rest, medicine, and lots of love and care to get better."

Mariam wanted to help. She asked, "Mama, Baba, can I help take care of Grandma Aisha?"

Fatima smiled and replied, "Yes, Mariam. You can help by being gentle and kind to her."

Every morning, Mariam went to Grandma Aisha's room with a big smile and said, "Good morning, Grandma! How are you feeling today?"

Grandma Aisha would smile and say, "Good morning, my dear Mariam. I feel a little better today, thank you."

Mariam helped her mother make soup for Grandma Aisha. She carefully carried the bowl to her grandmother and said, "Here, Grandma. I made you some soup. It will help you feel better."

Grandma Aisha smiled and said, "Thank you, Mariam. You are such a caring girl."

Every day after school, Mariam read stories to her grandmother. One afternoon, she read a story about a brave little bird. Grandma Aisha listened with a smile and said, "You read so well, Mariam. I enjoy your stories very much."

Mariam also helped her grandmother take her medicine. She would bring a glass of water and say, "Here, Grandma, it's time for your medicine."

One day, Mariam's friend, Aisha, came to visit and wanted to play outside. Mariam said, "I can't play right now. I need to take care of my grandmother."

Aisha understood and said, "That's very kind of you, Mariam. Your grandmother is lucky to have you."

One evening, Grandma Aisha said, "Mariam, you have been so kind and caring. You are like a little nurse, taking care of me so well."

Mariam felt proud and hugged her grandmother. "I love you, Grandma. I want you to get better soon," she said.

Mariam's parents were very proud of her. Her father, Ahmed, said, "Mariam, you are doing a wonderful job taking care of Grandma. The Prophet Muhammad (Sallallahu Alayhi Wasallam) taught us to be kind and take care of the sick."

Mariam listened carefully and felt even more determined to help. As days went by, Grandma Aisha started feeling better. One morning, she said, "Mariam, thanks to your care and kindness, I am feeling much better. You have been my little angel."

Mariam's heart filled with joy. She promised always to be kind and care for others, just like she had done for her grandmother.

Moral of the Story:

Show compassion and care for those who are sick, and always be kind to others.

Hadith:

The Prophet Muhammad (Sallallahu Alayhi Wasallam) said: "Whoever visits a sick person continues to remain in the fruit garden of Paradise until he returns." (Sahih Muslim, Hadith 2568)

Chapter 28

The Respectful Neighbor

THE RESPECTFUL NEIGHBOR

Once upon a time, in a small village, there lived a kind boy named Hassan. He loved playing outside and exploring. Hassan lived with his parents, Amina and Ali, in a cozy house, and they cared for all their neighbors.

One sunny morning, Hassan's mother, Amina, said, "Hassan, we are going to visit our neighbor, Mr. Rahim. He is an old man and needs our help." Hassan liked Mr. Rahim, who always told interesting stories. "Yes, Mama! I want to help!" Hassan replied.

They walked to Mr. Rahim's house and found him sitting in his garden, looking tired. Amina said, "Good morning, Mr. Rahim. We are here to help you with anything you need." Mr. Rahim smiled and said, "Thank you. I need help with my garden. The weeds are growing, and I can't pull them out."

Hassan said, "Don't worry, Mr. Rahim. I will help you!" Hassan and his mother started working in the garden. Hassan pulled out the weeds while Amina trimmed the bushes. Mr. Rahim smiled and said, "You are a kind boy, Hassan. Thank you for helping me."

After they finished, Mr. Rahim told Hassan a story about a neighbor who was always kind and helped others. Everyone loved him because of his kindness. Hassan listened and decided he wanted to be like the kind neighbor in the story.

The next day, Hassan saw his friend, Fatima, trying to reach a ball stuck in a tree. He ran over and said, "Let me help you, Fatima." Hassan climbed the tree and got the ball down. Fatima smiled and said, "Thank you, Hassan! You are a good friend."

One afternoon, Hassan saw their neighbor, Mrs. Layla, carrying heavy bags. She looked tired. Hassan quickly ran over and said, "Let me help you, Mrs. Layla." She smiled and said, "Thank you, Hassan. You are very kind." Hassan helped her carry the bags to her house. She said, "You are a helpful neighbor, Hassan. Thank you so much."

Hassan felt proud. He remembered a Hadith his father had told him: "The Prophet Muhammad (Sallallahu Alayhi Wasallam) taught us to care for our neighbors. He said, 'The best of neighbors in the sight of Allah is the best to his neighbor.'"

The next morning, Hassan saw Mr. Samir, an elderly man, planting flowers. Hassan ran over and said, "Good morning, Mr. Samir. Can I help you plant the flowers?" Mr. Samir smiled and said, "Thank you, Hassan. I would love your help." They worked together to plant the flowers. Mr. Samir said, "Thank you, Hassan. You are a kind neighbor."

Hassan felt happy helping his neighbors. He knew respecting and helping them was important and wanted to follow the teachings of the Prophet Muhammad (Sallallahu Alayhi Wasallam).

Hassan continued to help everyone around him, always greeting everyone with a smile. His neighbors loved him and appreciated his kindness. Hassan knew respecting and helping others made the world a better place.

Moral of the Story:

Always respect and help your neighbors.

Hadith:

The Prophet Muhammad (Sallallahu Alayhi Wasallam) said: "The best of companions in the sight of Allah is the best to his companion, and the best of neighbors in the sight of Allah is the best to his neighbor." (Tirmidhi, Hadith 1944)

Chapter 29

The Brave Protector

Once upon a time, in a small village, there lived a boy named Zayd. Zayd was kind and cheerful and always tried to help others.

One morning, on his way to school, Zayd saw his friend Amin looking sad. Zayd asked, "Amin, what's wrong?"

Amin replied, "Some boys made fun of me because I wear glasses."

Zayd felt sorry for his friend. "Don't worry, Amin. I will always stand by you," he said with a smile.

At school, Zayd saw the boys who teased Amin. They were laughing and pointing at him. Zayd walked over and said, "It's not nice to make fun of others. We should treat others how we want to be treated."

The boys were surprised and realized he was right. They apologized to Amin, who felt happy and thanked Zayd for standing up for him. During recess, Zayd and Amin played together, and Amin felt much better.

After school, Zayd's teacher, Mrs. Sara, called him to her desk. "Zayd, I saw how you stood up for Amin. That was very brave and kind," she said with a smile. Zayd felt proud.

That evening, Zayd's father, Ali, told him, "The Prophet Muhammad (Sallallahu Alayhi Wasallam) taught us to help those who are being treated unfairly. He said, 'Help your brother, whether he is an oppressor or is being oppressed.'"

Zayd asked, "Baba, how can I help someone being treated unfairly?"

His father replied, "You can help by standing up for them and being kind."

The next day, Zayd saw Fatima being teased by older kids who took her lunch. Zayd said, "That's not fair. Give Fatima her lunch back."

The older kids asked, "Why do you care?"

Zayd replied, "Because it's wrong to take someone's lunch. We should be kind."

The older kids thought about it and gave back Fatima's lunch. Fatima thanked Zayd for helping her.

Later, Zayd saw a little boy named Yusuf being chased by bigger kids who wanted his toy car. Zayd ran over and said, "Stop! Leave him alone!"

The bigger kids asked, "Why should we?"

Zayd replied, "Because it's not right to take someone's toy. We should play together and be friends."

The kids realized he was right, apologized, and invited Yusuf to play with them. Yusuf thanked Zayd.

Zayd was happy to help his friends and knew that standing up for others was the right thing to do. He wanted to keep being brave and kind, just like the Prophet Muhammad (Sallallahu Alayhi Wasallam) taught.

From that day on, Zayd always helped others and made sure everyone felt safe and happy. His friends loved him for his kindness and courage.

Moral of the Story:

Always stand up for and protect those who are vulnerable.

Hadith:

The Prophet Muhammad (Sallallahu Alayhi Wasallam) said: "Help your brother, whether he is an oppressor or is being oppressed." (Sahih Bukhari, Hadith 2444)

Chapter 30

The Truthful Witness

THE TRUTHFUL WITNESS

Once upon a time, in a small village, lived a young boy named Bilal. Bilal was known for his kindness and honesty, values his parents taught him. He loved playing with his friends and learning new things at school.

One morning, on his way to school, Bilal met his friend Hamza, who looked worried. "Bilal, I need your help!" Hamza exclaimed. "Someone broke the window at school, and the teacher thinks I did it, but I didn't!"

Knowing Hamza was a good boy, Bilal reassured him, "Don't worry, Hamza. Let's go to school and tell the teacher the truth."

When they arrived, they found their teacher, Mr. Ali, near the broken window. Bilal said, "Mr. Ali, Hamza didn't break the window. I saw what happened. A ball from the playground hit it, thrown by older kids. Hamza was with me the whole time."

Mr. Ali listened carefully and thanked Bilal for his honesty. Later, the older kids admitted their mistake and apologized. "Thank you for telling the truth, Bilal," they said. "We were afraid to admit it." Bilal replied, "It's okay. It's important to always tell the truth, even when it's hard." The kids agreed and promised to be more careful.

That evening, Bilal's father, Omar, said, "I heard what happened at school today. I am proud of you for telling the truth." Bilal smiled. His father added, "The Prophet Muhammad (peace be upon him) taught us that 'Truthfulness leads to righteousness, and righteousness leads to Paradise.' This means that being honest makes us good people." Bilal felt determined to always be truthful.

The next day, Bilal noticed his friend Aisha looking upset. He asked, "Aisha, what's wrong?" She replied, "Someone took my new pencil, and I need it for my homework." Bilal decided to help. He saw Youssef with a pencil that looked like Aisha's and asked, "Did you take Aisha's pencil by mistake?"

Youssef looked at the pencil and said, "Oh no, I think I did! I'm sorry, Aisha. I didn't realize it was yours." Aisha smiled and said, "Thank you, Youssef. I'm glad you told the truth." Bilal was happy to see his friends resolving the issue with honesty.

Another day, while playing soccer, Bilal and his friends accidentally broke a neighbor's flowerpot. Everyone looked worried, but Bilal knew what to do. He went to the owner and said, "I'm sorry, sir. We accidentally broke your flowerpot. It was an accident, and we didn't mean to do it."

The owner appreciated their honesty and said, "Thank you for telling the truth, Bilal. Accidents happen, but it's important to be truthful." Bilal felt proud and happy, remembering the teachings his father had shared.

Bilal continued to choose honesty, knowing it was always the right thing to do. He remembered the Hadith his father told him and felt proud to be a truthful person.

Moral of the Story:

Always be truthful and honest, even when it's difficult.

Hadith:

The Prophet Muhammad (Sallallahu Alayhi Wasallam) said: "Truthfulness leads to righteousness, and righteousness leads to Paradise. A man continues to speak the truth until he is recorded with Allah as a truthful person." (Sahih Bukhari, Hadith 6094)

Chapter 31

The Kind Teacher

Once upon a time, in a small village, there was a school with a kind teacher named Miss Sara. She loved her students and always tried to make learning fun. Miss Sara believed that teaching with love and kindness was very important.

One sunny morning, the children arrived at school excited for another day of learning. Miss Sara greeted each of them with a warm smile and a friendly "Good morning!"

In Miss Sara's class, there was a boy named Ahmed. Ahmed found reading very difficult and often felt sad because he couldn't read as well as his friends. One day, during reading time, Ahmed struggled with a word and felt tears in his eyes. Miss Sara noticed this and walked over to him.

"Ahmed, it's okay. Everyone learns at their own pace," she said gently. She sat next to him and helped him sound out the word. "Let's try this together," she encouraged. Ahmed felt better and tried again. With Miss Sara's help, he finally read the word correctly. "Thank you, Miss Sara!" he said, smiling.

Miss Sara smiled back and replied, "You're welcome, Ahmed. I'm very proud of you for trying your best."

Every day, Miss Sara helped her students with whatever they found difficult. She knew being patient and kind made them feel confident. She also made learning fun by using games and songs.

One afternoon, Miss Sara brought paints and paper for an art project. "Today, we will paint pictures of our favorite animals," she announced. The children cheered with excitement.

There was a girl named Fatima in Miss Sara's class. Fatima was very shy and didn't think she was good at painting. Miss Sara noticed Fatima sitting quietly and said, "Fatima, would you like to paint with me?"

Fatima nodded shyly and picked up a brush. Miss Sara showed her how to mix colors and make beautiful shapes. "You're doing a wonderful job, Fatima," Miss Sara said.

Fatima started to feel more confident and painted a lovely picture of a butterfly. She showed it to Miss Sara, who said, "This is beautiful, Fatima! You are a great artist." Fatima smiled brightly and felt proud of herself. She realized that with a little help and encouragement, she could do anything.

Miss Sara also loved telling stories. Every day, she gathered the children in a circle and read them a story. One day, she told a story about a brave little ant who helped his friends. After the story, she asked, "What did you learn?"

A boy named Zayd raised his hand and said, "I learned that we should always help our friends, just like the little ant."

"That's right, Zayd," Miss Sara said with a smile. "Helping others is very important."

Miss Sara's kindness and patience made a big difference. Her students felt safe and happy in her classroom. One day, they decided to make a special card for her. They drew pictures and wrote messages, saying, "Thank you, Miss Sara, for being the best teacher!"

Miss Sara was touched by their kindness. She hugged her students and said, "Thank you, my dear students. You are all wonderful, and I am proud of each of you."

Miss Sara knew that her kindness had a big impact. She shared a Hadith with her students: "The Prophet Muhammad (Sallallahu Alayhi Wasallam) said, 'The best among you are those who have the best manners and character.' This means being kind is very important."

Her students listened carefully and promised to always be kind and have good manners. They knew that following Miss Sara's example would make them better people.

From that day on, Miss Sara continued to teach with love and kindness, and her students always tried to be the best they could be.

Moral of the Story:

Being kind and patient makes learning fun and helps everyone feel happy and confident.

Hadith:

The Prophet Muhammad (Sallallahu Alayhi Wasallam) said: "The best among you are those who have the best manners and character." (Sahih Bukhari, Hadith 6029)

Chapter 32

The Patient Fisherman

Once upon a time, in a small village by the sea, there lived a kind fisherman named Ibrahim. He loved fishing on the calm waters. Ibrahim had a young son named Sami, who was curious and eager to learn about fishing.

One sunny morning, Ibrahim decided to take Sami on a fishing trip. Sami was very excited. "Baba, I want to catch the biggest fish in the sea!" he exclaimed.

Ibrahim smiled. "Remember, Sami, fishing requires patience. Sometimes we have to wait a long time before we catch a fish."

Sami nodded, but he was too excited to understand. They gathered their fishing gear and set off. At their favorite spot, Ibrahim showed Sami how to bait the hook and cast the line into the water.

Sami watched and tried to do the same. They sat quietly in the boat, watching the waves. After a few minutes, Sami asked, "Baba, why haven't we caught any fish yet?"

Ibrahim replied, "Be patient, Sami. The fish will come when the time is right. We just have to wait."

Sami tried to sit still but kept looking at the water. As time passed, he grew more impatient. "Baba, can we move to another spot?" he asked.

Ibrahim shook his head. "Patience, my son. The fish are here. We just need to give them time."

Sami sighed but trusted his father. They continued to wait, enjoying the peaceful sea. Suddenly, Ibrahim felt a tug on his line. "Sami, look! I think we have a fish!" he said.

Sami watched as his father carefully reeled in the line. A big, beautiful fish appeared. "Wow, Baba! It's so big!" Sami exclaimed.

Ibrahim smiled. "See, Sami? Patience pays off. If we had moved, we might have missed this fish."

Sami nodded. "I see, Baba. I'll try to be more patient."

They continued fishing, and Sami practiced patience. After a while, he felt a small tug on his line. "Baba, I think I caught a fish!" he said excitedly.

Ibrahim watched as Sami reeled in the line. A small fish appeared. "I did it, Baba! I caught a fish!" Sami said proudly.

Ibrahim hugged him. "You did a great job, Sami. Patience helped you succeed."

On the way back, Ibrahim told Sami a story. "The Prophet Muhammad (Sallallahu Alayhi Wasallam) taught us about patience. He said, 'Patience is a light.' This means that being patient helps us see things clearly."

Sami listened and felt proud to learn from his father and the teachings of the Prophet. He promised to remember the lesson about patience.

When they returned home, Sami told his mother, Amina, about their trip. "Mama, I learned about patience today!" he said.

Amina smiled. "That's wonderful, Sami. I'm very proud of you."

From that day on, Sami practiced patience in everything he did.

Moral of the Story:

Patience helps us achieve our goals and see things more clearly.

Hadith:

The Prophet Muhammad (Sallallahu Alayhi Wasallam) said: "Patience is a light." (Sahih Muslim, Hadith 223)

Chapter 33

The Grateful Traveler

Once upon a time, in a small village, there lived a boy named Hasan. Hasan was a cheerful child who loved adventures. One day, his parents, Mr. and Mrs. Khan, decided to take him on a special trip to visit his grandparents in a distant village.

Hasan was very excited. He packed his favorite toys, some snacks, and his backpack. "Mama, Baba, I'm ready! Let's go!" he said eagerly.

They set off early in the morning with their donkey. Mr. Khan led the donkey while Mrs. Khan and Hasan walked beside him. Hasan admired the tall trees, green fields, and colorful flowers along the way.

After a while, Hasan felt tired. "Are we there yet, Baba?" he asked.

Mr. Khan smiled and said, "Not yet, Hasan. It's a long journey, but let's enjoy the beautiful sights around us."

Hasan nodded and watched the birds and animals. "Look, Mama! There are cows and sheep!" he exclaimed.

Mrs. Khan replied, "Yes, Hasan. Nature is beautiful, and we should be thankful for everything we see."

They stopped for a break by a river and had a picnic. Hasan enjoyed the fresh air and the sound of the water. "This is so nice, Mama. I'm thankful we stopped here," he said.

Mrs. Khan hugged him. "I'm glad you're enjoying it, Hasan. It's important to be thankful."

After their break, they continued their journey. But soon, their donkey stopped and wouldn't move. "Oh no, what happened, Baba?" Hasan asked.

Mr. Khan checked the donkey. "It looks like our donkey needs a rest," he said. "We'll have to wait a bit."

Hasan felt a little upset but remembered to be thankful. He asked, "Baba, can I help you take care of the donkey?"

Mr. Khan smiled. "Of course, Hasan. Thank you for helping."

They gave the donkey water and rested. After a while, the donkey was ready to go. "Good job, Hasan. I'm proud of you," Mr. Khan said.

Finally, they reached their grandparents' village. Hasan saw his grandparents waiting with big smiles. "Grandma! Grandpa!" he shouted with joy.

His grandparents hugged him. "Welcome, Hasan! We're so happy to see you," they said.

Hasan felt happy and grateful to be with his family. They spent days exploring, playing games, and listening to stories from his grandparents. Hasan enjoyed every moment and remembered to be thankful.

One evening, Grandma said, "Hasan, the Prophet Muhammad (Sallallahu Alayhi Wasallam) taught us that 'He who does not thank the people is not thankful to Allah.' This means we should always be grateful."

Hasan felt determined to be thankful. On the way home, he thought about all he was grateful for: his parents, the beautiful nature, his grandparents, and the things he learned.

When they reached home, Hasan hugged his parents and said, "Thank you, Mama and Baba, for the wonderful trip. I'm very thankful for everything."

Mr. and Mrs. Khan hugged him back and said, "We're proud of you, Hasan, for being such a grateful and happy traveler."

From that day on, Hasan continued to be thankful every day, always remembering to appreciate the kindness of others.

Moral of the Story:

Always be thankful and show gratitude for what you have and the people who help you.

Hadith:

The Prophet Muhammad (Sallallahu Alayhi Wasallam) said: "He who does not thank the people is not thankful to Allah." (Tirmidhi, Hadith 1954)

Chapter 34

The Responsible Gardener

THE RESPONSIBLE GARDENER

Once upon a time, there was a small village called Naranj. In this village, lived a young boy named Ramin. Ramin loved playing outside, especially in the garden behind his house.

One sunny morning, Baba Reza called Ramin over. "Ramin, today I will teach you how to be a responsible gardener. It's important to care for our garden because it gives us food, clean air, and beauty."

Ramin nodded eagerly. "Yes, Baba! I want to learn!"

Baba Reza smiled and gave Ramin a small clay jug. "First, we need to water the plants. Plants need water to grow strong and healthy."

Ramin carefully poured water on the flowers and vegetables. "Look, Baba! The plants are happy!" he exclaimed.

"Yes, Ramin," said Baba Reza. "But we must not waste water. We should use just enough to keep the plants healthy."

Next, Baba Reza showed Ramin how to pull out the weeds. "Weeds take nutrients from the soil. We must remove them so our plants can grow better."

Ramin pulled out the weeds with his small hands. It was hard work, but he felt proud when he saw the clean soil around the plants.

As they worked, Baba Reza talked about composting. "When leaves fall or we have vegetable scraps, we can turn them into compost. Compost is like food for the soil."

"How do we make compost, Baba?" asked Ramin.

"We collect leaves, grass, and vegetable scraps in a pile," Baba Reza explained. "Then we let them break down and turn into rich soil. This soil is very good for our garden."

Ramin helped Baba Reza gather leaves and scraps for the compost pile, excited to see how they would turn into soil.

After a while, they took a break under a big tree. Baba Reza said, "Taking care of the garden also means protecting our environment. We should not throw waste carelessly and must keep our surroundings clean."

Ramin asked, "What should we do with waste, Baba?"

"We should put vegetable scraps in the compost pile. For things that cannot break down, like broken pots, we keep them in a safe place," Baba Reza replied.

Ramin decided to collect all the broken tools at home and store them safely. He felt happy knowing he was helping the environment.

That evening, as the sun set, Ramin said, "Baba, I feel like I did something very important today."

Baba Reza hugged him. "You did, my son. You learned to be a responsible gardener and to care for the earth. Allah has entrusted us with this duty."

Ramin felt proud to be a steward of the earth. From that day on, he worked hard to care for the garden, knowing he was fulfilling an important duty.

Moral of the Story:

We should take care of the earth and our environment because it is our responsibility.

Hadith:

The Prophet Muhammad (Sallallahu Alayhi Wasallam) said: "The world is green and beautiful, and Allah has appointed you as His stewards over it." (Sahih Muslim, Hadith 2742)

Chapter 35

The Joyful Journey of Learning

THE JOYFUL JOURNEY OF LEARNING

Once upon a time, in the village of Gulistan, lived a bright boy named Javad who loved to learn. Every day, he ran to the village school, excited to see his friends and his teacher, Ustad Karim. Ustad Karim was a wise and kind teacher who often said, "Learning is a joy, and knowledge is a treasure."

One morning, Ustad Karim told the children, "Today, we will learn about the stars." Javad's eyes lit up. "I love looking at the stars! They are so beautiful," he said.

"Did you know that the stars are like faraway suns?" Ustad Karim asked. "Each star is a sun in its part of the universe."

Javad asked, "How do we know that stars are suns?"

"Long ago, people used telescopes to study the stars and found they are made of the same things as our sun," Ustad Karim explained. "By learning and exploring, we discover amazing things."

Javad felt happy. He loved learning and sharing his new knowledge with his family.

One day, Ustad Karim brought a globe to class. "Today, we will learn about different places in the world," he said.

Javad was excited to learn about other countries. Ustad Karim pointed to the globe and told stories about the pyramids in Egypt, the Great Wall of China, and many other places.

That evening, Javad drew a picture of the globe and showed it to his family. "Look, this is our Earth! I learned so much today!" he said proudly.

His father smiled and said, "Javad, remember, seeking knowledge is important and should bring you joy."

Another day, Ustad Karim told a story about a wise man who loved learning. "This man traveled far to seek knowledge with a cheerful heart, knowing that knowledge is a gift from Allah," he said.

Javad said, "I want to seek knowledge with a cheerful heart too."

"That is wonderful, Javad," replied Ustad Karim. "The Prophet Muhammad (Sallallahu Alayhi Wasallam) said, 'The angels lower their wings for the seeker of knowledge.' When you learn with happiness, even the angels honor you."

Inspired by these words, Javad went to school every day with a smile, eager to learn. His friends saw his joy and began to find happiness in learning, too.

One afternoon, Javad saw a butterfly and ran to tell Ustad Karim. "Look, a butterfly with colorful wings!" he said.

"Did you know butterflies start as caterpillars and change to become butterflies?" asked Ustad Karim.

"That's amazing! I want to learn more," Javad exclaimed.

"Always remember," said Ustad Karim, "there is so much to learn, and when you seek knowledge with joy, the journey is even more beautiful."

Javad felt happy, knowing he would always seek knowledge with joy and share it with others. He became known as the cheerful student who loved to learn.

Moral of the Story:

Learning is a joy, and seeking knowledge with a cheerful heart makes the journey beautiful.

Hadith:

The Prophet Muhammad (Sallallahu Alayhi Wasallam) said: "The angels lower their wings for the seeker of knowledge, out of pleasure for what he does." (Sunan Ibn Majah, Hadith 226)

Chapter 36

The Humble Scholar

Once upon a time, in the peaceful village of Nooristan, there lived a wise scholar named Farhad. Farhad loved to read books, learn new things, and teach others. Many students came from far and wide to learn from him.

Every morning, Farhad would sit under a big, shady tree with his books, greeting his students with a warm smile. One of his favorite students was a curious boy named Kamran who loved asking questions.

One day, Kamran asked, "Teacher, why do you always smile and speak kindly to everyone?"

Farhad replied, "Kamran, it is important to be humble and kind. No matter how much we know, there is always more to learn. We should never think we are better than others because of our knowledge."

Kamran asked, "But Teacher, everyone respects you. How do you stay humble?"

Farhad told him a story, "Once, a wise man was asked, 'How do you know so much?' He replied, 'My knowledge is like a drop of water in the vast ocean. There is always more to learn.'"

Kamran understood. "So, no matter how much we know, we should always keep learning?"

"Yes, Kamran," said Farhad. "When we are humble, we can learn from everyone and everything around us."

One sunny morning, Farhad took Kamran and the other students on a walk through the village. They visited the market, the river, and the fields. Farhad pointed out different things and asked questions.

At the market, he asked, "What can we learn from the people here?"

Kamran said, "We can learn how to trade and be fair."

Farhad nodded. "And we can learn about hard work and honesty."

Next, they went to the river. Farhad asked, "What can we learn from the river?"

A student replied, "The river teaches us to be adaptable and go with the flow."

Farhad smiled. "Yes, and it also teaches us patience and perseverance."

Finally, they visited the fields. Farhad asked, "What can we learn from the farmers?"

Kamran answered, "We can learn about planting seeds, taking care of crops, teamwork, and helping each other."

Farhad was pleased. "You are learning well. Remember, knowledge is everywhere. Always stay humble and open to learning."

Kamran felt deep respect for his teacher. He realized that being a true scholar meant being humble and always willing to learn.

From that day on, Kamran worked hard to learn with humility. He helped his friends and treated everyone with kindness. He knew that no matter how much he learned, there was always more to discover.

Moral of the Story:

No matter how much we know, we should always stay humble and be willing to learn more.

Hadith:

The Prophet Muhammad (Sallallahu Alayhi Wasallam) said: "The best among you are those who learn the Quran and teach it." (Sahih Bukhari, Hadith 5027)

Chapter 37

The Just King

Once upon a time, in the land of Saffronia, there was a young king named Arash. He had just become king after his father, King Darius. Arash wanted to be a good and fair ruler like his father.

One day, King Arash asked his wise advisor, Hakim, "How can I rule with fairness and make everyone in my kingdom happy?"

Hakim replied, "Your Majesty, a just king listens to his people and is kind and humble. When you listen with an open heart, you will find the wisdom to make fair decisions."

King Arash decided to visit the village to hear what his people had to say. He put on simple clothes and went to the marketplace. He saw a long line of people waiting to talk to the judge and joined them to listen.

An old woman named Fatima said, "My neighbor's cow ate all the vegetables in my garden. Now I have nothing to sell at the market."

The neighbor, Hassan, admitted, "Yes, my cow broke through the fence and ate her vegetables. I am sorry, but I have no money to pay her back."

The judge decided, "Hassan, you must help Fatima replant her garden and share half of your cow's milk with her until the vegetables grow back."

King Arash was impressed by the fair decision and continued listening to more cases, learning about justice.

The next day, he returned to the palace and announced, "From now on, we will have open court days where anyone can come and speak to me directly."

People from all over the kingdom came to speak with King Arash. One day, a farmer named Bahram complained, "My neighbor's sheep keep eating my crops, and he won't fix his fence."

King Arash called the neighbor, Reza, to the court. Reza explained, "My fence is broken, and I have no money to fix it."

King Arash decided, "Reza, you must fix your fence, and Bahram, you will help him. Reza, you will share some wool with Bahram until his crops grow back." Both men agreed and felt happy with the fair decision.

King Arash continued to listen to his people and made fair decisions. He learned that being a just king meant treating everyone with kindness, humility, and fairness.

One day, Hakim said, "Your Majesty, you are doing a wonderful job. Remember the words of our beloved Prophet Muhammad (Alayhis Salaam), who said, 'The just will be seated upon pulpits of light.' (Sahih Muslim 1827). You are following this Hadith by ruling with fairness."

King Arash felt happy and promised to continue ruling with fairness and kindness. In the land of Saffronia, he became known as the just king who made his kingdom a happy and peaceful place.

Moral of the Story:

Treat everyone with kindness and fairness, and always listen with an open heart.

Hadith:

The Prophet Muhammad (Sallallahu Alayhi Wasallam) said: "The just will be seated upon pulpits of light." (Sahih Muslim, Hadith 1827)

Chapter 38

The Generous Farmer

Once upon a time, in a small village called Darband, there lived a kind farmer named Karim. Karim loved working on his farm, growing vegetables, fruits, and grains. Every year, he had a bountiful harvest because he took good care of his plants and animals.

One sunny morning, Karim saw that his vegetables were ripe, his fruit trees were full, and his grain fields were ready to harvest. He was very happy and thanked Allah for the blessings. Karim thought, "I have more than enough for my family. What should I do with the extra harvest?" He remembered his wise grandfather's words: "Sharing brings joy and blessings."

Karim decided to share his harvest with his neighbors. He filled baskets with fresh vegetables, fruits, and grains and loaded them onto his cart. He visited his neighbors one by one.

First, he went to Ahmad's house. Ahmad was an elderly man living alone. "Salam, Ahmad! I brought you some fresh vegetables and fruits," Karim said.

Ahmad was surprised and happy. "Thank you, Karim! This is very kind of you. I was worried about getting food for the week. May Allah bless you!"

Karim felt happy and continued to visit his neighbors. He shared with Fatima, a widow with three children, and Zainab, who was sick and couldn't work in her garden. He even gave sweet apples and pears to the children playing in the street.

As Karim walked back to his farm, he felt joyful. He realized that sharing his harvest brought happiness to his neighbors and himself. That evening, his neighbors came to thank him and brought him gifts like fresh bread and handmade crafts. They sat together, sharing stories and laughter.

One of his neighbors, Hamid, said, "Karim, you have shown us the true meaning of generosity. Your kindness has brought us all together."

Karim replied, "I am happy to share what I have. It brings me joy to see everyone happy. We should always help each other and share our blessings."

The next day, Karim's son, Ali, asked, "Baba, why did you give away so much of our harvest? Don't we need it?"

Karim gently explained, "Allah has blessed us with more than we need. It is our duty to share with those who have less. When we share, we make others happy and feel happy too. Generosity brings joy to everyone."

Ali nodded and said, "I want to be generous like you, Baba."

Karim hugged his son and said, "That's wonderful, Ali. Remember that sharing and helping others is a good deed that brings us closer to Allah."

The village of Darband became known for its kind and generous people. Everyone helped each other and shared their blessings, filling the village with happiness.

And so, Karim became known as the generous farmer who brought joy to everyone around him.

Moral of the Story:

Sharing and being generous brings joy to everyone, and it is a good deed that makes our hearts happy.

Hadith:

The Prophet Muhammad (Sallallahu Alayhi Wasallam) said: "The best charity is that which is given when one is self-sufficient, and start by giving first to your dependents." (Sahih Bukhari, Hadith 1426)

Chapter 39

The Compassionate Nurse

THE COMPASSIONATE NURSE

Once upon a time, in the small village of Shifaa, there lived a kind nurse named Layla. Layla loved helping people and always had a big smile. She worked at the village clinic, taking care of anyone who was sick or hurt.

One morning, Layla arrived at the clinic early. She put on her white nurse's uniform and got ready to see the patients. Soon, a young boy named Hassan walked in. He had hurt his knee while playing outside.

Layla knelt down and asked, "What happened, Hassan?"

Hassan replied, "I fell while running, and my knee hurts."

Layla gently led Hassan to a chair, cleaned his wound, and put a bandage on it. "There you go, Hassan. You are very brave!"

Hassan smiled. "Thank you, Nurse Layla. You are very kind."

Just then, Mr. Ali, an old man, came in holding his arm. Layla quickly helped him sit down. "What happened, Mr. Ali?"

Mr. Ali said, "I slipped while working in my garden and hurt my arm."

Layla examined his arm and said, "It looks like a sprain. I will wrap it up, and you should rest it for a few days."

Mr. Ali smiled and said, "Thank you, Layla. You are always so caring."

Throughout the day, Layla treated many patients, helping with cuts, bruises, and fevers. Everyone left feeling better, not just because of the treatment but because of Layla's kindness.

One evening, Layla's friend Fatima, who was also a nurse, visited the clinic. She said, "Layla, you are always so kind and gentle with everyone. How do you stay so compassionate?"

Layla replied, "I remember the words of the Prophet Muhammad (Alayhis Salaam): 'Show mercy to those on earth, and the One in the heavens will show mercy to you.' (Sunan Abi Dawud 4941). I believe that being kind and merciful is very important."

The next day, a young girl named Aisha came to the clinic with a fever. Layla gave her medicine and held her hand. "Don't worry, Aisha. You will feel better soon," she said softly.

Aisha whispered, "Thank you, Nurse Layla. You are like an angel."

Layla felt warmth in her heart and stayed by Aisha's side until her fever went down. She made sure Aisha was comfortable and had everything she needed.

As time passed, more people came to the clinic, and Layla continued to care for them with love. She knew that her gentle touch and kind words were just as important as the medicine she gave.

And so, in the village of Shifaa, Layla became known as the compassionate nurse who cared for everyone and spread kindness wherever she went.

Moral of the Story:

Being kind and compassionate to others is very important and brings joy to both the giver and the receiver.

Hadith:

The Prophet Muhammad (Sallallahu Alayhi Wasallam) said: "Show mercy to those on earth, and the One in the heavens will show mercy to you." (Sunan Abi Dawud, Hadith 4941)

Chapter 40

The Brave Soldier

Once upon a time, in the land of Ajnad, there lived a brave soldier named Tariq. Tariq was known throughout the kingdom for his courage and strong heart. He always protected his people and stood up for what was right.

One day, the king called Tariq to the palace. "Tariq," the king said, "our kingdom is in danger. An enemy is planning to attack our village. We need your bravery to defend our people."

Tariq bowed and said, "Your Majesty, I will do everything I can to protect our village."

The king smiled. "I trust you, Tariq. May Allah be with you."

Tariq gathered his soldiers and prepared for battle. He spoke to them, "My friends, we must be brave and protect our village. We will fight with all our strength and courage."

The soldiers felt inspired by Tariq's words. They knew that with Tariq leading them, they could win.

As the sun began to set, the enemy soldiers approached. Tariq stood at the front of his army, holding his sword. He told his soldiers, "Remember, courage is not the absence of fear, but the strength to face it. Let's protect our home and families."

The battle began, and Tariq fought bravely, defending his fellow soldiers. The enemy was strong, but Tariq's courage never wavered. He knew he had to protect his village.

During the battle, Tariq saw a young soldier named Bilal struggling against an enemy. Bilal was scared and ready to give up. Tariq rushed to his side and shouted, "Bilal, do not be afraid! Be brave and fight!"

Bilal felt stronger and fought back with all his might. Together, Tariq and Bilal pushed the enemy back, showing great bravery.

As night fell, the enemy began to retreat. They could not match the bravery of Tariq and his soldiers. The village was safe, and the people cheered for their heroes.

The next morning, the king came to the battlefield. He saw the bravery of Tariq and his soldiers and was proud. "Tariq, you have shown great courage and brought honor to our kingdom."

Tariq bowed and said, "Thank you, Your Majesty. It was our duty to protect our people."

The king declared a feast to celebrate the victory. The villagers honored Tariq and his soldiers, singing songs of bravery.

During the feast, Bilal thanked Tariq. "Your courage gave me strength," he said.

Tariq smiled. "Bilal, you were brave too. Remember, courage is within all of us."

Tariq spoke to the villagers, "Today, we have shown that courage can overcome any challenge. Let us always be brave and stand up for what is right."

The villagers promised to follow Tariq's example of bravery. And so, in the land of Ajnad, Tariq became a hero, inspiring everyone to be brave and strong.

Moral of the Story:

Courage is not the absence of fear, but the strength to face it. We should always be brave and stand up for what is right.

Hadith:

The Prophet Muhammad (Sallallahu Alayhi Wasallam) said: "The best of your leaders are those whom you love, and who love you, and you pray for them, and they pray for you." (Sahih Muslim, Hadith 1821)

Chapter 41

The Patient Tailor

THE PATIENT TAILOR

Once upon a time, in a small village, there lived a kind and patient tailor named Hamid. He was known for making the most beautiful clothes in the village. Hamid's shop was always busy because he took his time and did his best work.

One morning, a young boy named Ali came to Hamid's shop. Ali wanted to learn how to be a tailor. He knocked on the door and said, "Assalamu Alaikum, Hamid. Can you teach me how to be a tailor?"

Hamid smiled and replied, "Wa Alaikum Assalam, Ali. I will teach you, but you must be patient and work hard. Tailoring takes time to learn."

Ali eagerly agreed. Hamid gave him a piece of cloth and some thread. "First, we will learn to sew a straight line," he said. Ali tried, but his stitches were crooked and uneven. He sighed and said, "Hamid, this is too hard."

Hamid patted his shoulder and said, "Don't worry, Ali. It is hard at first, but with patience and practice, you will get better."

Ali took a deep breath and continued sewing. Day after day, he practiced, and with Hamid's help, his stitches became neater and straighter. He was happy to see his progress.

One day, Hamid gave Ali a new task. "Now, you will learn to sew buttons on a shirt. This takes patience," he said. Ali tried, but the buttons kept falling off. Frustrated, he said, "This is too difficult!"

Hamid smiled and said, "Remember, we must be patient. Take your time and do it carefully." Ali tried again, more slowly this time, and the buttons stayed in place. He felt proud of his work.

As the days passed, Ali learned more about tailoring. He learned to measure cloth, cut patterns, and sew different stitches. He practiced every day and became better, always remembering Hamid's words about patience.

One day, a rich man came to the shop and asked Hamid to make a special suit. "I need this suit to be perfect," he said.

Hamid smiled and replied, "It will take time, but I will make it perfect."

Hamid and Ali worked on the suit together. They measured the cloth carefully, cut the patterns precisely, and sewed with great care. It took many days, but they did not rush. They wanted the suit to be perfect.

When the rich man came to try it on, he was very happy. "This is perfect!" he said. "Thank you, Hamid. You have done a wonderful job."

Hamid replied, "Thank you. It was all possible because of patience and hard work." Ali felt proud. He had learned that being patient and taking time to do things properly was very important.

As Ali continued to learn from Hamid, he remembered to be patient in everything he did. He knew that patience helped him improve, and one day, he hoped to be as good a tailor as Hamid.

Moral of the Story:

Patience helps us do our best work.

Hadith:

The Prophet Muhammad (Sallallahu Alayhi Wasallam) said: "The best of you are those who are best in their dealings with others." (Sahih Bukhari, Hadith 6063)

Chapter 42

The Grateful Farmer

THE GRATEFUL FARMER

Once upon a time, in a small village, there lived a kind farmer named Karim. Karim had a big farm where he grew crops like wheat, corn, and vegetables. Every day, he worked hard, planting seeds, watering plants, and taking care of the soil. Karim loved his farm and always thanked Allah for giving him the strength to work.

One sunny morning, Karim went to his farm. He looked at the clear, bright sky and said, "Alhamdulillah, thank you, Allah, for this beautiful day."

Karim checked his wheat fields. The wheat had grown tall and golden, ready for harvest. "Alhamdulillah, thank you, Allah, for the good wheat," he said with a smile.

Next, he went to his cornfield. The corn plants were strong, and the corn cobs were big and ready to be picked. Karim picked a corn cob and said, "Alhamdulillah, thank you, Allah, for the good corn."

Then, Karim visited his vegetable garden. The tomatoes, cucumbers, and carrots were ripe and ready. He tasted a tomato, found it sweet and juicy, and said, "Alhamdulillah, thank you, Allah, for the good vegetables."

Karim felt grateful for his bountiful harvest and decided to thank Allah in a special way. He went to the mosque and prayed, "O Allah, thank you for the good wheat, corn, and vegetables. Thank you for blessing my farm. Alhamdulillah."

After praying, Karim returned to his farm and began harvesting. He cut the wheat and tied it into bundles, saying, "Alhamdulillah, thank you, Allah, for the good wheat." He picked the corn, saying, "Alhamdulillah, thank you, Allah, for the good corn." He harvested the vegetables, saying, "Alhamdulillah, thank you, Allah, for the good vegetables."

Karim's farm was full of good crops, and he was happy. He knew that Allah had blessed him because he worked hard and was grateful. He decided to share his harvest with the villagers.

Karim loaded his cart with wheat, corn, and vegetables and went to the village. "Come, my friends, and share the good harvest that Allah has blessed us with," he called out.

The villagers came, saw the harvest, and were very happy. They thanked Karim for sharing. Karim smiled and said, "Alhamdulillah, thank you, Allah, for the good harvest."

One day, a young boy named Hasan came to learn from Karim. Karim welcomed him and said, "I will teach you, but remember to always be grateful for everything that Allah gives us."

Hasan nodded and promised to be grateful. Karim taught him how to plant seeds, water the plants, and care for the soil. Hasan worked hard and always thanked Allah for the good crops.

Soon, Hasan became a good farmer too. He shared his crops with the villagers, and they thanked him for his kindness. Karim was proud of Hasan and said, "Alhamdulillah, thank you, Allah, for everything."

Moral of the Story:

Always be thankful for what you have.

Hadith:

The Prophet Muhammad (Sallallahu Alayhi Wasallam) said: "The best of people are those who bring the most benefit to mankind." (Sahih Bukhari, Hadith 6022)

Chapter 43

The Responsible Student

THE RESPONSIBLE STUDENT

Once upon a time, in a small village, there was a young boy named Yusuf. Yusuf loved playing with his friends, but he also knew that learning was important. He went to school every day and had a kind teacher named Mr. Ahmad who always encouraged the students to study hard.

One morning, Mr. Ahmad told the class, "Children, it is very important to study with dedication and work hard."

Yusuf listened carefully. He wanted to be a good student and make his parents proud. At home, he told his parents what Mr. Ahmad had said. His mother smiled and said, "Yusuf, your teacher is right. Studying helps us learn new things and become better people."

Yusuf decided to study diligently. He made a plan to study every day after school and do all his homework on time. The next day, he went to school with a big smile, excited to learn new things.

During the math lesson, Mr. Ahmad asked a difficult question. Yusuf raised his hand and answered correctly. Mr. Ahmad was pleased and said, "Well done, Yusuf! You have been paying attention and studying hard."

Yusuf felt happy because his hard work was paying off. He continued to do his homework right away and read his books. He enjoyed learning and felt proud of himself.

One day, Mr. Ahmad asked the class to write an essay about what they wanted to be when they grew up. Yusuf wrote about his dream of becoming a doctor. "I want to be a doctor to help people," he wrote. "I will study hard to learn everything I need to know."

Mr. Ahmad read Yusuf's essay and was impressed. "Yusuf, you have written a wonderful essay," he said. "If you continue to study with dedication, you will become a great doctor."

Yusuf felt proud. He knew that studying hard was helping him reach his dreams.

One afternoon, Yusuf's friend Ali asked him to play outside. Yusuf wanted to play but remembered his promise to study first. He said, "Ali, I need to finish my homework. I will join you later."

Ali was surprised, but Yusuf explained, "It's important to be responsible and do our homework first. We can play afterward." Yusuf finished his homework and then joined his friends, feeling happy because he had done the right thing.

As time went by, Yusuf continued to study hard and became very good in his studies. Mr. Ahmad often praised him in class. One day, Mr. Ahmad shared a Hadith: "The Prophet Muhammad (Alayhis Salaam) said, 'Whoever follows a path in the pursuit of knowledge, Allah will make a path to Paradise easy for him.' (Sahih Muslim 2699)."

Yusuf shared this Hadith with his family, saying, "Seeking knowledge is very important. We must all study diligently."

His parents were proud of him. Yusuf knew that being a responsible student was the key to success. He continued to study hard and became one of the top students in his class.

Yusuf was happy and grateful. He knew that with dedication and hard work, he could achieve anything he wanted.

Moral of the Story:

Always study hard and be responsible.

Hadith:

The Prophet Muhammad (Sallallahu Alayhi Wasallam) said: "Whoever follows a path in the pursuit of knowledge, Allah will make a path to Paradise easy for him." (Sahih Muslim, Hadith 2699)

Chapter 44

The Cheerful Neighbor

THE CHEERFUL NEIGHBOR

Once upon a time, in a small village, lived a cheerful girl named Layla. Layla loved to make people happy and believed that spreading joy was one of the best things anyone could do. She lived with her parents in a cozy house with friendly neighbors.

One sunny morning, Layla woke up with a big smile. She decided to spread happiness to everyone she met.

Layla decided to start by visiting Mrs. Khan, an elderly lady next door. Mrs. Khan loved flowers, so Layla picked some daisies from her garden, put them in a small vase, and knocked on Mrs. Khan's door.

Mrs. Khan opened the door and smiled. "Good morning, Layla! What a lovely surprise!" she said.

"Good morning, Mrs. Khan! I brought you some flowers to make you smile," Layla said cheerfully.

Mrs. Khan hugged Layla. "Thank you, dear. You have made my day brighter," she said with a warm smile.

Feeling happy, Layla continued to school. On the way, she saw Mr. Ali struggling to carry a heavy box. Layla ran up and offered to help.

"Good morning, Mr. Ali! Can I help you with that box?" she asked.

Mr. Ali was grateful. "Thank you, Layla. That's very kind of you," he said. Together, they carried the box into his garage. "You are such a helpful girl, Layla," Mr. Ali said, smiling.

At school, Layla greeted her friends and shared her snacks with those who didn't have any. Her friends were happy and thanked her for her kindness.

After school, Layla saw her friend Sara sitting alone, looking sad. Layla asked, "What's wrong, Sara?"

Sara replied, "I lost my favorite pencil and can't do my homework."

Layla smiled and said, "I have an extra pencil you can use." She handed Sara a colorful pencil.

Sara's face lit up. "Thank you, Layla! You always know how to make me feel better," she said.

On her way home, Layla saw her neighbor, Mr. Hamid, planting flowers. She waved and said, "Good afternoon, Mr. Hamid! Your garden looks beautiful!"

Mr. Hamid smiled. "Thank you, Layla! You always bring joy to our neighborhood," he said.

That evening, Layla's parents praised her. "Layla, you have done a wonderful job spreading happiness today. We are very proud of you," her mother said.

Layla smiled and said, "I just want to make everyone happy."

Layla felt proud and happy. She knew spreading joy was a kind act and a way to follow the teachings of the Prophet Muhammad (Sallallahu Alayhi Wasallam). From that day on, Layla continued to spread happiness wherever she went, making her neighborhood a brighter place.

Moral of the Story:

Always try to spread joy and happiness to those around you. A small act of kindness can make a big difference.

Hadith:

The Prophet Muhammad (Sallallahu Alayhi Wasallam) said: "The best of people are those who bring the most benefit to mankind." (Sahih Bukhari, Hadith 6014)

Chapter 45

The Humble Artisan

THE HUMBLE ARTISAN

Once upon a time, in a small village, there lived a kind artisan named Hamza. Hamza was known for making beautiful pottery—pots, vases, and bowls that everyone admired. People from near and far came to buy his creations.

Every morning, Hamza woke up early and went to his workshop. He loved working with clay, shaping it carefully into wonderful pieces. As he worked, he always thanked Allah for giving him the skill to create such beautiful things.

One day, Hamza's friend, Ali, visited him and saw the beautiful pottery. "Hamza, your work is amazing! You are the best potter in the village," Ali said.

Hamza smiled and replied, "Thank you, Ali. I am grateful for the skills Allah has given me, but it is important to be humble and not boast about our skills."

Ali asked, "Why is it important to be humble?"

Hamza explained, "Being humble means not thinking we are better than others. It means using our skills to help others without bragging. When we are humble, we can learn more and become better people."

Ali nodded and understood. He watched Hamza carefully shape a beautiful vase with patience and care.

One sunny day, the village had a big market. Hamza decided to take his pottery to sell. He packed his pots, vases, and bowls and went to the market with Ali.

At the market, people admired Hamza's pottery and praised his work. Hamza smiled humbly and thanked them. He did not boast but said, "Alhamdulillah, I am thankful for the talent Allah has given me."

Later, a wealthy merchant named Mr. Kareem came to Hamza's stall. "This is beautiful work! I would like to buy all of your pots and vases," he said.

Hamza was surprised and happy. "Thank you, Mr. Kareem. I hope my work brings you joy," he replied.

Mr. Kareem smiled and said, "You are very humble, Hamza. Many would boast if they had your skills, but you are different."

Hamza replied, "It is important to stay humble. The Prophet Muhammad (Sallallahu Alayhi Wasallam) said, 'Whoever humbles himself for the sake of Allah, Allah will raise him in status.' (Sahih Muslim 2588). I try to live by these words every day."

Mr. Kareem was impressed by Hamza's wisdom and promised to come back for more pottery. Hamza continued to serve his customers with a smile.

As the sun set, Hamza and Ali packed up and went home. Ali said, "Hamza, I learned today that being humble is a great virtue. You are a wonderful example of humility and kindness."

Hamza smiled and said, "Thank you, Ali. Always remember to be grateful for your skills and use them to help others."

When they reached home, Hamza's family was proud of him, not just for his beautiful pottery but for his humble heart.

Moral of the Story:

Always be humble and grateful for your skills. Humility makes us better people and brings us closer to Allah.

Hadith:

The Prophet Muhammad (Sallallahu Alayhi Wasallam) said: "Whoever humbles himself for the sake of Allah, Allah will raise him in status." (Sahih Muslim, Hadith 2588)

Chapter 46

The Loving Friend

Once upon a time, in a small village, there lived a kind boy named Hassan. Hassan loved helping others and had a best friend named Amir. They did everything together—played games, studied, and shared snacks. They were like brothers.

One sunny morning, Hassan was excited because it was Amir's birthday. He wanted to make it special, so he decided to give Amir his favorite wooden toy horse. Although Hassan loved the toy, he knew it would make Amir very happy.

Hassan wrapped the toy in colorful paper and went to Amir's house. When Amir opened the gift, his eyes lit up. "Thank you, Hassan! This is the best gift ever!" he said, hugging Hassan. Hassan felt happy seeing Amir's joy. He remembered a Hadith his mother taught him: "The Prophet Muhammad (Sallallahu Alayhi Wasallam) said, 'None of you truly believes until he loves for his brother what he loves for himself.'" (Sahih Bukhari 13).

After giving the gift, Hassan and Amir went to the park to play. They saw a little boy sitting alone, crying. Hassan and Amir asked, "Why are you sad?"

The boy replied, "I lost my toy and have nothing to play with."

Hassan wanted to help. He looked at Amir, and Amir nodded. Hassan took out a small ball from his backpack and gave it to the boy. "Here, you can have this ball," he said.

The boy's face brightened. "Thank you! Now I can play too," he said happily. Hassan and Amir invited the boy to play with them. They had fun together, and Hassan felt happy knowing he had made someone smile.

Throughout the day, Hassan and Amir spread kindness. They helped an old lady carry her groceries and shared snacks with a hungry dog. Each time they helped someone, they felt a warm feeling inside, knowing they were doing the right thing.

That evening, Hassan told his mother about his day. She smiled and said, "You did a wonderful job, Hassan. You showed great compassion and love for others."

Hassan replied, "I remembered the Hadith you taught me, Mom. 'None of you truly believes until he loves for his brother what he loves for himself.' I tried to follow it today."

His mother hugged him and said, "I am very proud of you."

The next day, at school, Hassan and Amir saw the boy from the park again. This time, he was smiling and playing with other children. He waved at Hassan and Amir, and they waved back, knowing they had made a new friend.

As days passed, Hassan and Amir continued to be kind and loving friends. They helped each other with homework, shared their toys, and made sure no one felt left out. Their friendship grew stronger, and they became known as the most caring friends in the village.

Hassan felt happy knowing he was following the teachings of the Prophet Muhammad (Sallallahu Alayhi Wasallam) by showing love and compassion to others.

Moral of the Story:

Always show love and compassion to your friends. Love for others what you love for yourself.

Hadith:

The Prophet Muhammad (Sallallahu Alayhi Wasallam) said: "None of you truly believes until he loves for his brother what he loves for himself." (Sahih Bukhari, Hadith 13)

Chapter 47

The Just Judge

THE JUST JUDGE

Once upon a time, in a small village, there lived a wise and kind judge named Zayd. Judge Zayd was known for being fair and always listening carefully to everyone. The people trusted him because he was honest and just. Judge Zayd remembered the words of the Prophet Muhammad (Sallallahu Alayhi Wasallam): "Allah loves those who are just." (Sahih Muslim 2588).

One sunny morning, Judge Zayd went to the village court to help solve problems. The first case was between two neighbors, Mr. Ali and Mr. Ahmed. They were arguing about a tree between their houses. Mr. Ali said the tree was his, while Mr. Ahmed said it was his.

Judge Zayd listened to both of them and thought carefully. He suggested, "Why don't you share the tree? You can take turns enjoying its shade and picking its fruits." Mr. Ali and Mr. Ahmed smiled and agreed. They realized that sharing the tree was a good idea. Judge Zayd was happy to see them become friends again.

The second case was about a shopkeeper named Mr. Hassan and a customer named Mrs. Fatima. Mrs. Fatima bought a bag of rice from Mr. Hassan, but the rice was old and not good to eat. She asked for a refund, but Mr. Hassan refused.

Judge Zayd listened to both sides and examined the rice. He said, "Mr. Hassan, it is not right to sell old rice. You must be honest in your business. Please give Mrs. Fatima a refund and check your products before selling them."

Mr. Hassan felt ashamed and apologized to Mrs. Fatima. He promised to be more careful in the future. Mrs. Fatima smiled and thanked Judge Zayd, feeling happy that justice was served.

Later, a young boy named Bilal came to the court. Bilal was sad because his friends were not sharing their toys with him. Judge Zayd advised, "Bilal, it is important to be fair and kind to each other. Share your toys, and your friends will share with you."

Bilal nodded and promised to talk to his friends about sharing. Judge Zayd was glad to see Bilal learning the importance of fairness.

As the sun set, Judge Zayd remembered the Hadith that guided his actions: "Allah loves those who are just." He felt grateful for the wisdom to make fair decisions and knew that being a just judge was a way to help his community and follow the teachings of the Prophet Muhammad (Sallallahu Alayhi Wasallam).

The next day, Judge Zayd returned to the court, ready to listen and help the villagers again. He knew that being fair and just was the key to a happy and peaceful village.

Moral of the Story:

Always be fair and just in your decisions. Justice makes our community strong and peaceful.

Hadith:

The Prophet Muhammad (Sallallahu Alayhi Wasallam) said: "Allah loves those who are just." (Sahih Muslim, Hadith 2588)

Chapter 48

The Kind Cook and the Hungry People

THE KIND COOK AND THE HUNGRY PEOPLE

Once upon a time, in a small village, there was a cook named Amir. Amir loved to cook and made the tastiest meals in the village. Everyone loved his fresh and delicious food.

One day, Amir went to the market to buy vegetables and fruits. He saw some children sitting by the road, looking sad and hungry. Amir asked, "Why do you look so sad?"

A little boy replied, "We are hungry. We have not eaten anything today."

Amir felt sorry for the children and said, "Come with me to my kitchen. I will cook a big meal for you."

The children followed Amir to his kitchen. Amir started cooking right away. He chopped vegetables, stirred pots, and added spices. The kitchen filled with delicious smells. Soon, he had made a big pot of soup, some warm bread, and a sweet dessert. He served the food to the children, who ate happily.

After they finished eating, a little girl said, "Thank you, Amir. You are very kind."

Amir smiled and replied, "I am glad you enjoyed the food. Always remember to help others when you can."

Word spread quickly about Amir's kindness. More hungry people came to his kitchen. Some were old, some were young, and some were families. Amir welcomed everyone and made sure no one went hungry.

One day, a man named Farid came to Amir's kitchen. Farid was very poor and had no money to buy food. He asked, "Can you please give me something to eat?"

Amir smiled and said, "Of course, Farid. You are always welcome here." He gave Farid a warm bowl of soup and some bread. Farid thanked Amir with tears in his eyes.

As days passed, Amir's kitchen became known as a place where anyone could come and eat. People from nearby villages also came to taste Amir's delicious food. Amir never turned anyone away. He believed in sharing and helping those in need.

One cold winter evening, a traveler named Salma came to Amir's door. She was tired and hungry after a long journey. Amir welcomed her warmly and said, "Please sit down and rest. I will prepare a meal for you."

Salma was grateful and watched Amir cook with care and love. Amir served her a hot meal, and she thanked him for his kindness. "Your heart is as warm as your food, Amir," Salma said.

Amir replied, "It is my pleasure to help. Everyone deserves a warm meal and a kind heart."

One day, a little boy named Karim came to Amir's kitchen and said, "My family is very poor. We have no food at home. My mother is sick, and my little sister is hungry."

Amir packed a basket with bread, soup, fruits, and sweets. He gave it to Karim and said, "Take this to your family. I hope your mother feels better soon."

Every day, Amir cooked and shared his food with those in need. His kitchen was always full of laughter and joy.

A wise old man once told Amir, "You are like a shining star in our village." Amir felt shy and replied, "I am just doing what I can to help."

Amir continued to cook and feed the hungry, knowing that sharing his food made the world a better place. His kitchen was a symbol of kindness and generosity.

Moral of the Story:

Always help others and share what you have. It makes the world a happier place.

Hadith:

The Prophet Muhammad (Sallallahu Alayhi Wasallam) said: "The best charity is to satisfy a hungry person." (Sunan Ibn Majah, Hadith 3664)

Chapter 49

The Honest Farmer

THE HONEST FARMER

Once upon a time, in a peaceful village called Nurabad, lived a kind and hardworking farmer named Karim. Karim had a small piece of land where he grew vegetables and fruits. Every day, he worked hard, plowing the fields, planting seeds, and watering the plants. Karim loved his farm and always thanked Allah for giving him the strength to work.

Karim had a young son named Amin who loved helping him on the farm. Amin would carry water, pick vegetables, and feed the animals. One sunny morning, as they worked together, Karim decided to teach Amin an important lesson about honesty.

"Amin, my son," Karim began, "today, I want to tell you a story about honesty in farming."

Amin's eyes sparkled with curiosity. He loved listening to his father's stories.

"Many years ago," Karim continued, "there was a farmer like me. This farmer was known for his honesty. He never cheated or lied about his work. One day, he found a large, beautiful pumpkin in his field, the biggest he had ever seen!"

Amin imagined the giant pumpkin and listened eagerly.

"Instead of keeping it for himself," Karim went on, "the farmer took it to the market. He knew the pumpkin would fetch a good price, but he didn't want to overcharge. He weighed it and set a fair price. When people saw the pumpkin, they were amazed and asked if it was really from his farm. The farmer replied, 'Yes, I grew it with my own hands and took good care of it.'"

Karim paused and asked, "Do you know what happened next?"

Amin shook his head. "What happened, Baba?"

"The people trusted him because he was always honest," Karim explained. "They bought the pumpkin and praised him for his fairness. Soon, more people came to buy from him. His farm prospered, and he became known as the most trustworthy farmer in the village."

Amin nodded thoughtfully. "Baba, I want to be like that farmer. I want to be honest and work hard."

Karim smiled. "That's my boy! Honesty is very important, especially in farming. We must always give people what we promise and never cheat them."

As they continued working, Karim showed Amin how to plant seeds properly and take care of the soil. "Farming is hard work, Amin," Karim said. "But when we do it honestly, Allah rewards us."

One day, Amin found some weeds in the garden. He thought about pulling them out quickly, but he remembered his father's words. He carefully removed each weed, making sure not to harm the plants.

Karim noticed Amin's effort and smiled. "You are learning well, my son. Remember, honesty is not just about words; it's also about our actions."

Weeks passed, and the farm flourished. When they took their produce to the market, Karim said, "Amin, today you will sell our vegetables. Be honest with the customers."

Amin was excited. He greeted the customers with a smile, weighed each item carefully, and gave fair prices. An elderly man watched him and said, "Young man, you are honest. Keep up the good work."

At the end of the day, they returned home with an empty cart. Karim hugged his son and said, "I am proud of you, Amin. You have learned the value of honesty."

Amin smiled, knowing he would always follow his father's teachings and be an honest farmer.

Moral of the Story:

Always be honest and do your work with integrity. Honesty makes people trust you, and it brings blessings from Allah.

Hadith:

The Prophet Muhammad (Sallallahu Alayhi Wasallam) said: "Whoever believes in Allah and the Last Day, let him speak good or remain silent." (Sahih Muslim, Hadith 47)

Chapter 50

The Brave Leader

Once upon a time, in the beautiful village of Safa, there lived a brave and wise leader named Tariq. He was known for his courage and fairness, always standing up for what was right. His people loved and respected him deeply.

Tariq had a young son named Yusuf, who admired his father and dreamed of becoming a great leader like him one day.

One day, while walking through the village, Tariq and Yusuf noticed a group of villagers looking worried. Yusuf tugged at his father's sleeve and asked, "Baba, why do the people look so worried?"

Tariq knelt down to Yusuf's level and replied, "My son, there seems to be a problem in the village. The river that gives us water is drying up, and the people are afraid they won't have enough water for their families and farms."

Yusuf's eyes widened with concern. "Baba, what are we going to do?"

Tariq smiled and said, "Do not worry, Yusuf. A good leader must stay calm and think of a solution. Let us go talk to the villagers and find out more."

They approached the crowd, and the villagers explained that the river had been slowly drying up for weeks. Tariq listened carefully and then spoke in a strong, reassuring voice. "Dear friends, we must not lose hope. I will lead a group to find out what is causing this and fix it. Together, we can solve this problem."

The villagers felt comforted by Tariq's words, trusting that he would help them.

Tariq gathered a group of strong villagers to investigate the river upstream. Yusuf wanted to join, but Tariq asked him to stay back to help the villagers remain calm. "Yusuf, being a leader also means helping others feel safe and hopeful. Stay here and support our friends while we find the solution."

Yusuf nodded, understanding. "I will do my best, Baba."

Tariq and his team traveled for days, following the river through rocks and forests until they found a large dam built by beavers, blocking the water's flow. They spoke to the beavers and explained the village's problem. The beavers agreed to help, and together, they worked hard to remove the dam, allowing the river to flow freely again.

Back in the village, Yusuf kept everyone's spirits up by sharing stories of his father's bravery and encouraging them to stay hopeful. He helped distribute the little water they had left, ensuring everyone had enough to drink.

After many days, Tariq and his team returned with the good news that the river was flowing again. The villagers cheered and celebrated as the water filled their wells and watered their fields.

Tariq hugged Yusuf and said, "You did a wonderful job, my son. You helped the villagers stay hopeful and brave. That is the mark of a true leader."

Yusuf beamed with pride, knowing that one day, he would grow up to be a great leader just like his father.

Moral of the Story:

A brave leader stays calm in difficult times and always looks for solutions. Leading with courage and love helps everyone feel safe and hopeful.

Hadith:

The Prophet Muhammad (Sallallahu Alayhi Wasallam) said: "The best of your leaders are those whom you love, and who love you, and you pray for them, and they pray for you." (Sahih Muslim, Hadith 1824)

www.ingramcontent.com/pod-product-compliance
Lightning Source LLC
Chambersburg PA
CBHW082337300426
44109CB00045B/2402